LIVING PRAYER

Living Prayer

A Book of Hours for Renewing Creation

Alison M. Benders
Lisa Fullam
Gina Hens-Piazza

LITURGICAL PRESS
Collegeville, Minnesota

litpress.org

Cover image courtesy of Getty Images.

Scripture quotations are from New Revised Standard Version Bible © 1989 National Council of the Churches of Christ in the United States of America. Used by permission. All rights reserved worldwide.

© 2024 by Alison M. Benders, Lisa Fullam, and Gina Hens-Piazza

Published by Liturgical Press, Collegeville, Minnesota. All rights reserved. No part of this book may be used or reproduced in any manner whatsoever, except brief quotations in reviews, without written permission of Liturgical Press, Saint John's Abbey, PO Box 7500, Collegeville, MN 56321-7500. Printed in the United States of America.

1	2	3	4	5	6	7	8	9

Library of Congress Cataloging-in-Publication Data

Names: Benders, Alison M., author. | Fullam, Lisa, author. | Hens-Piazza, Gina, 1948– author.
Title: Living prayer : a book of hours for renewing creation / Alison M. Benders, Lisa Fullam, Gina Hens-Piazza.
Description: Collegeville, Minnesota : Liturgical Press, [2024] | Summary: "In the tradition of the liturgy of the hours, Living Prayer offers a four-week cycle of morning and evening prayer to support a more sustainable lifestyle. Created with ecological and social justice-oriented individuals and organizations in mind, Living Prayer supports hands-on work in local communities. The book also includes a variety of green rituals to extend ecological prayer"— Provided by publisher.
Identifiers: LCCN 2024009072 (print) | LCCN 2024009073 (ebook) | ISBN 9798400801372 (trade paperback) | ISBN 9798400801389 (epub) | ISBN 9780814688892 (pdf)
Subjects: LCSH: Creation—Religious aspects—Christianity. | Human ecology—Religious aspects—Christianity. | Social justice—Religious aspects—Christianity. | BISAC: RELIGION / Prayerbooks / Christian | RELIGION / Christianity / Catholic
Classification: LCC BT695 .B433 2024 (print) | LCC BT695 (ebook) | DDC 264/.15—dc23/eng/20240326
LC record available at https://lccn.loc.gov/2024009072
LC ebook record available at https://lccn.loc.gov/2024009073

In gratitude for all JST students, who over the years have shown us what renewal and rebirth look like in their studies and their ministries.

CONTENTS

Introduction   ix

Week One   **Let There Be Life!**
Celebrating the Gift of Creation   1

Week Two   **Ruptured Relationships**
Acknowledging Our Alienation   51

Week Three   **Healing Creation**
Accepting Christ's Salvation   109

Week Four   **Establishing the Renewed Creation**
Cultivating Life   159

Conclusion   **Cultivating Life for Renewing Creation**   211

Appendix   **Green Rituals and Practices**   215

INTRODUCTION

> For as the rain and the snow come down from heaven,
>   and do not return there until they have watered the earth,
> making it bring forth and sprout,
>   giving seed to the sower and bread to the eater,
> so shall my word be that goes out from my mouth;
>   it shall not return to me empty,
> but it shall accomplish that which I purpose,
>   and succeed in the thing for which I sent it.
>
> For you shall go out in joy,
>   and be led back in peace;
> the mountains and the hills before you
>   shall burst into song,
>   and all the trees of the field shall clap their hands.
>
> —Isaiah 55:10-12

The bountiful life on our planet ought to startle us and humble us. It is sacred. Whether we search the mystery of the starry blue heavens or gaze into the eyes of our beloved, the unsearchable loveliness of creation takes our breath away. Humanity's earliest poetry and songs express full-throated wonder for creation and thanksgiving to its transcendent Source. *Let there be life!* The most startling aspect of creation is life itself. Our awe extends particularly to the sacredness of creatures who are *imago dei*, in the image of God. Intuitively we recognize that life reveals the Holy One. God imbues life with sacred depth. In all living creatures we encounter the Spirit of God. We are drawn into God's infinitely tender love alive in the cosmos all around us.

As Isaiah proclaims in the passage that opens this Book of Hours, God's word goes forth to create life inexorably and abundantly, and creation responds with lush growth and fruitful bounty. How should we respond as a human community to the divine gifts of creation, life, and love? Most simply, we can give thanks in our words and actions. We can care for our common home, sharing its fruits with one another. As our gratitude flows naturally toward God, our hearts will join with God's heart. God's love will wash over us when we pray as participants in God's ecology of peace and plenty. But we have often failed to respond to God's gracious gift of life. We take greedy advantage of what creation offers, selfish and indifferent to the impact our actions have on the environment and on our fellow human beings.

Pope Francis's encyclical *Laudato Si': On Care for Our Common Home* lays out the intersecting social, natural, and economic crises that face all of us across the planet today. Reading the signs of our times, we recognize the escalating catastrophe as creation groans under the weight of humanity's sinful exploitation. Because of the inseparable bond between nature and the human community, the exploitation of our common home disproportionately devastates the poorest among us. The pope emphasizes that the environmental crisis at its foundation is a human spiritual crisis, which can only be addressed by our conversion to love one another. Through dialogue and commitment, people can amplify God's grace by nurturing an integral ecology where all life thrives through bonds of kinship and solidarity.

The interior work to care for our common home begins when we turn back to God seeking to be renewed in Christ as the first step toward renewing creation. This volume supports the conversion, the *metanoia*, that fosters a new way of living in the world. *Living Prayer: A Book of Hours for Renewing Creation* presents a four-week prayer cycle that begins and ends with life. Its method is formation through recitation, repetition, and reflection, following spiritual practices from earliest Christianity and Judaism. By *living prayer* through morning and evening hours, we strive to change our hearts and become conformed to the good news of God's abundant life. Its invitatory couplet voices our deepest longing: "Giver of Life, animate our hearts; inspire us to renew your creation."

Throughout this prayer cycle, the prayers use the expression "the ecology of God" instead of "kingdom" or "reign" of God. This expression finds its meaning in the notion from *Laudato Si'* of integral ecology. "Ecology of God" is more inclusive of the whole of creation and evokes the main theme of *Living Prayer*, which is the renewal of creation in, through, and with the renewal of human relationships. Care and generosity are the dynamism and *logos* of the ecology of God; gifts multiply and bear fruit. Human flourishing is rooted in gift. We thrive as a human community when we freely share with each other the love and life we receive from God. In the ecology of God, community and magnanimity supplant domination and exploitation. In God's ecology, Divine Breath stirs creation, rousing it from the dark abyss. Waters shower the land to bring forth plenty. The Word of God lives among us, healing and mending our fractured lives. All creation is renewed in unison, in communion with the Trinity. Our lives are secure in the ecology of God.

The *Living Prayer* Cycle

To use Pope Francis's words from *Laudato Si'*, we are "fatally alienated" from other human beings and from our common home. We need to be reformed and renewed to claim our role to cultivate creation with God. The pilgrimage of *Living Prayer* recapitulates the salvation story, beginning with creation, through humanity's alienation from God and nature, to our conversion and redemption, and leading finally to the risen Christ in whom we will dwell as one body, one community. *Living Prayer* opens our hearts to creation as the medium of God's love for us and of our free and loving response. The cycle forms and transforms us by nurturing in us a yearning for a renewed creation, where all tears will be wiped away—and all things will be united in Christ. By the repeating verses and through the poignancy of the psalms prayed daily, we find the words to express how all life is interwoven. We surrender our hearts to God's ecology.

Week One, *Let There Be Life!*, celebrates God's creation. We are invited to see the stories from Genesis with new eyes focused on the intertwined relationships in the ecology of God. The morning readings from the Hebrew Scriptures recapitulate the miracle of creation with Wisdom at God's side. The evening gospel readings amplify and extend the creation story by connecting it to Jesus, the Word through whom God created the cosmos. The intercessions and reflections help us contrast our reverence for creation with the overbuilt environment and suffering world that shape our experience today.

In Week Two, *Ruptured Relationships*, the Hebrew Bible readings carry the story of humanity's threefold alienation. We listen to stories of our alienation from nature, human community, and God. In the evening readings, Jesus' teachings underline humanity's ruptured relationships. No one on earth can be blind to the disintegration of life in the first decades of the twenty-first century. A community organized as *imago dei* in the ecology of God ought to be ordered by generosity, justice, and mercy, particularly for the poor. This week reveals through readings, reflections, and prayers how our indifference, resistance, and selfishness have caused a "fatal alienation" between God and humanity, between the environment and human society, and ultimately a chasm between individual people and human communities.

Week Three, *Healing Creation*, brings us back to God, just as Christ's passion, death, and resurrection initiates a new covenant. Progressing through this week, we move from alienation and despair to incipient hope by trusting Christ. As ever, our reconciliation with God in creation and in community is a response to God's grace that initiates healing when we have lost our way. Jesus embodies the law of love and gift that grounds the ecology of God. This week's scripture passages and prayers form us for our role in the healing and redemption of the world. We can recognize ourselves as Christ's hands and hearts to soothe and mend all life in God's ecology.

Finally, in *Establishing the New Creation*, Week Four celebrates the "already-but-not-yet" of the eschaton of a renewed creation. The readings show us how the new covenant, which is dawning in our hearts and actions, will extend to the ends of the earth. The ecology of God embraces all creation, forging an indestructible bond between life and peace. Here, the Spirit of Life comes to the fore to enkindle in us practices of kinship and solidarity. Because we are never relieved of our responsibility to cultivate the new earth with God, the readings and reflections of this week joyfully celebrate the divine-human collaboration, echoing the Genesis joy and God's delight at the dawn of time. This joy impels us to rededicate our lives to caring for our common home and ushering in the ecology of God.

Using *Living Prayer*

Living Prayer replicates the ancient spiritual pattern of the liturgy of the hours, with readings and prayers for morning and evening moments in a four-week cycle. Since prayer is intimate communication with God, the hours of *Living Prayer* can be adapted and amended in any way that will help to bring people into the presence of God. Personal and group adaptations might include music and song, special readings, meditation on an icon, or praying in nature where the Divine feels especially present.

The moments of the prayer here follow the traditional patterns for any Divine Office:

- *Opening greeting*: As with any sacred moment, we are invited to gather our energy and collect ourselves as we turn our hearts to God. Beginning with a few deep breaths is ideal for *Living Prayer*. In such centering breaths, we pay attention to the physical sensations in our limbs and our organs, and then release any burdens we carry. We can also silence our chattering thoughts, which fearfully promote or defend our fragile selves. In a silence beyond words, our hearts open to the vibrant web of compassion that binds us to each other in the life of the cosmos.

Generally, participants might begin each devotion with the sign of the cross. In addition to such a gesture of presence and recollection, a chime can signal time to gather and attend. A lit candle might symbolize the presence of the Spirit in our midst. Burning incense might signify the sweetness of prayers rising to God. Here is space for a group to select or design symbols that meaningfully gather them into the divine presence. The appendix of "Green Rituals and Practices" offers many possibilities to supplement the prayer hours and carry our intentions into daily life.

- *Invitatory couplet*: Each prayer period follows a similar formula, beginning with the invitatory couplet for the whole cycle: "Giver of Life, animate our hearts; inspire us to renew your creation." People familiar with the traditional liturgy of the hours may wish to retain the morning verse "O Lord, open my lips / And my mouth will declare your praise," or the evening verse "O God, come to my assistance. / O Lord, make haste to help me." In any case, with daily repetition, any invitatory couplet will summon our hearts to focus on the Source of Life and the nature of the cosmos as a generous gift.

- *Psalms and readings*: The psalms selected for *Living Prayer*, along with the responsorial verses, express the theme of the week. For example, in Week One, the psalmist's words express amazement, delight, and gratitude for the gift of creation, while those in Week Two emphasize despair and alienation to reflect humanity's exploitation of creation and one another. After each psalm, participants are prompted with the opening word of the doxology, "Glory . . . ," which a group can pray together to bring the psalm to a close. The traditional "Glory to the Father and to the Son and to the Holy Spirit" works well, or participants might elect a doxology that hews more closely to the themes of the prayer cycle here, such as "Glory to the Creator, the Savior, and the Sustainer," or other words of praise.

The readings for morning prayer come from the Hebrew Scriptures, while those for evening prayer are drawn from the New Testament. In group settings, one member may be appointed to proclaim God's word for all present. The selected readings narrate the Christian story of creation as the most fundamental gift of a loving God, a gift which humanity has despoiled but which is recreated anew in and through the risen Christ. Participants should feel free to add or substitute readings from the Christian scriptures or any other spiritual traditions that express their understanding of the sacredness of all life.

- *Reflection*: At the evening prayer only, a question is posed for reflection. Participants are invited to consider the weekly theme in light of that day's readings or to seek God's presence in new moments and situations. Similar to the Ignatian examen, reflection is appropriate at the day's end, as we harvest the day's graces and commend ourselves into God's hands for our nightly rest. The reflection questions can be used for individual meditation, as a homily prompt for the community, or for group sharing.

- *Intercessions and the Lord's Prayer*: The purpose of the intercessions is to pray for God's people and all creation. A brief invocation precedes the intercessions, but participants are welcome to personalize the prayers to align with their community's needs. The Lord's Prayer closes out each movement of morning and evening prayer, using the words that Jesus taught his disciples.

In this prayer, participants might be invited to speak to the Lord in any language that feels most natural, or the language of intimacy for them.

- *Sign of peace*: Near the close of each hour participants are invited to offer a sign of peace. The sign varies for each week, with a gesture that captures the spirit of the week and signifies communion with the natural world. These gestures are recommended whether participants are praying alone or in the company of others. Week One invites us to open our palms wide to welcome creation; during Week Two, our bowed heads and folded hands signify contrite hearts; in Week Three we open our arms to welcome the hope of redemption; and in Week Four we greet creation's renewal with hands raised to the heavens. As a final option, when a group is praying through *Living Prayer*, more traditional gestures of welcome and peace can be adopted according to the group's preferences. As a spiritual practice, when we use gestures daily, offering them throughout the days and weeks, our whole being becomes an enfleshed invocation of divine presence and blessing.

- *Closing blessing*: After the sign of peace, the closing blessing sums up the hour and sends the community forth. It draws upon themes from the daily readings or the week, and can be amended to speak to the community's particular circumstances and needs.

As with traditional liturgies of the hours, the weekly cycle of *Living Prayer* begins with Sunday as the Lord's

Day, the first day of the week. Sunday is always a day of celebration and hope because of Christ's resurrection. These hours continue the ancient tradition, so the psalms, readings, and prayers on Sundays proclaim joy and confidence in God. Fridays, according to the Christian tradition, are days of penitence in remembrance of Jesus' crucifixion on Good Friday. Thus, in this *Living Prayer* cycle, the Friday themes will be more somber and reflective. They urge us to recognize how our personal failure to live generously contributes to the degradation of our common home and injures others. The remaining days narrate the week's theme, so participants are encouraged to read and reflect with an eye to recognizing the sweep of God's cosmic project and our role, good and bad, in the revelation of created love.

If it is not possible to pray all four weeks of morning and evening hours, we offer these suggestions. For a weeklong retreat, participants might select the week that aligns with the liturgical season (e.g., for Ordinary Time, select Week One; for Lent, select Week Two; for Advent, select Week Three; and for Easter through Pentecost, select Week Four, or Three and Four). If *Living Prayer* will be used for a briefer retreat, the hours for Friday through Sunday might be used, transitioning from one week to the next through penitence to joy. Additional green rituals or practices can be added to any morning or evening hour. Supplemental readings on particular climate-justice topics or Catholic social teaching, even *Laudato Si'*, can help draw participants deeper in the challenges humanity faces in cultivating an integral ecology.

Hope for a Renewed Creation

The invitatory couplet of *Living Prayer* speaks of deep hope: "Giver of Life, animate our hearts; inspire us to renew your creation." These few words express our faith that God is continually renewing all creation for us and with us; such is the destiny of the cosmos. We long to thrive, fully alive, on that promised day, which Christian tradition names the resurrection. We can recognize that day to come as the ecology of God, where care for our common good intersects with care for our common home.

What will it take for creation to be renewed? It will take each one of us converting our hearts and hands to the ecology of God. Through this *Living Prayer* cycle, we offer our own lives to sanctify, nurture, and heal our planet and life all around us. God's nature and life are generosity beyond measure. When our lives overflow with generosity in the image of God, we hasten the renewal of creation. This is our hope. Let us pray through our lives.

WEEK ONE

LET THERE BE LIFE!

Celebrating the Gift of Creation

Creation reveals God's endless abundance arrayed in the sparkling heavens, fixed in ancient stones, and swirling in the ocean depths. Flowering trees and fruitful vines cover the land. An infinite variety of beasts, birds, and bugs fill every planetary habitat from the tundra to the equator. While human beings share life in common with other creatures, the Giver of Life invites people to be co-creators, to tend and nurture the garden of creation. From the dawn of creation, God invites and entrusts us to be cultivators of life and community without limit so that we might share in the divine cosmic delight.

The morning readings this week resound with the creative Word summoning all life into existence. Wisdom herself witnesses the grandeur of these majestic beginnings, and the prophet Isaiah likewise praises the glory of God visible in creation. These familiar passages thrum with the language of breath, light, fecundity, quenching, and flourishing. The hills bedecked with flowers proclaim the joy of being alive. Even God stands in awe of all that has come into being. As we contemplate these gifts of creation, we are also summoned to remember our role as servant-cultivators of the divine handiwork.

The evening texts focus upon the creative power of God's word now manifest as the incarnate Word, Jesus. The prologue to John's Gospel reminds us that Jesus was with God at the beginning and recalls that Jesus is the light that overcomes the darkness of all eras and ruptures. And despite the worries of our lives, Jesus' parable about the lilies teaches us to abide in him and have confidence in his care for us. The accompanying psalms this week summon all of life to admire and give thanks for the wonders of creation. Thus, as we recite these hymns, our voices join a chorus with the rest of the living creatures offering collective praise to our God.

With new technologies, we attempt to grasp the immensity of our earth, the planets, and newly revealed galaxies. This week, as we contemplate the gifts of creation, our hearts turn to God's infinite grandeur. Our efforts to comprehend the Creator falter, yet fill us with sincere humility and reverence. And even more astounding, the God-Mystery invites us into a personal relationship. Jesus shows us the way to God, while the Holy Spirit embraces us with love and strengthens us to respond.

WEEK ONE

SUNDAY MORNING

✝

Giver of Life, animate our hearts;
inspire us to renew your creation.

PSALM 19:1-4, 14
℟ The heavens tell the glory of God; all creation sings for joy.

The heavens are telling the glory of God;
   and the firmament proclaims his handiwork.
Day to day pours forth speech,
   and night to night declares knowledge.
There is no speech, nor are there words;
   their voice is not heard;
yet their voice goes out through all the earth,
   and their words to the end of the world. . . .

Let the words of my mouth and the meditation of my heart
   be acceptable to you,
   O Lord, my rock and my redeemer.

Glory . . .

SCRIPTURE   Genesis 1:1-5

In the beginning when God created the heavens and the earth, the earth was a formless void and darkness covered the face of the deep, while a wind from God swept over the face of the waters. Then God said, "Let there be light"; and there was light. And God saw that the light was good; and God separated the light from the darkness. God called the light Day, and the darkness he called Night. And there was evening and there was morning, the first day.

The word of the Lord.

INTERCESSIONS

O God, you are the source of life and light. At your command the cosmos came to be. Day after day, sunlight pours through our atmosphere to energize the cycles of life and growth that sustain all life on this planet. We also marvel at the stars that sprinkle the night sky, so silent and deep. And so we pray: *Gracious God, renew our hearts to love your world.*

- Awaken us to experience humanity's connection to the earth and the integral ecology that gives us life. *We pray to the Lord.*

- Foster in the nations a respect for science, and for all those who study the world and its workings. *We pray to the Lord.*

- Enlighten the nations with wisdom for a just plan to heal the beautiful world that you entrusted to our care. *We pray to the Lord.*

THE LORD'S PRAYER
With these petitions in our hearts, we pray as our brother Jesus taught us: Our Father . . .

SIGN OF PEACE
As a sign of peace, Living God, we offer to you our palms wide open, ready to receive your gift of light and love. May your peace rest on us.

CLOSING PRAYER
God is no longer remote or hidden from us. The revelation of life and love begins with God's first word into creation: "Let there be light." May the God of light open our eyes to the splendor of creation as we walk through our day in hope and trust. We ask this in Christ's name. AMEN

WEEK ONE

SUNDAY EVENING

Giver of Life, animate our hearts;
inspire us to renew your creation.

PSALM 111:1-4
℟ The heavens tell the glory of God; all creation sings for joy.

Praise the Lord!
I will give thanks to the Lord with my whole heart,
 in the company of the upright, in the congregation.
Great are the works of the Lord,
 studied by all who delight in them.
Full of honor and majesty is his work,
 and his righteousness endures forever.
He has gained renown by his wonderful deeds;
 the Lord is gracious and merciful.

Glory . . .

SCRIPTURE   Matthew 5:13-16
[Jesus said to them:] "You are the salt of the earth; but if salt has lost its taste, how can its saltiness be restored? It is no longer good for anything, but is thrown out and trampled under foot.

"You are the light of the world. A city built on a hill cannot be hid. No one after lighting a lamp puts it under the bushel basket, but on the lampstand, and it gives light to all in the house. In the same way, let your light shine before others, so that they may see your good works and give glory to your Father in heaven."

The Gospel of the Lord.

REFLECTION
What opportunities have been present for us today to revere God's creation?

INTERCESSIONS
O God, before the cosmos, beyond the dark and light, you are. In the hustle and bustle of our daily concerns, we shield our eyes from the beautiful things you have made. It is too wonderful for us to grasp. And so we pray: *Gracious God, renew our hearts to love your world.*

- May we raise our children to revere creation by teaching them well about the natural world. *We pray to the Lord.*
- Help us to stop in our busy day to be aware as we inhale the sweet air that sustains us. *We pray to the Lord.*
- Give us the courage to fight for the preservation of wild spaces. *We pray to the Lord.*

THE LORD'S PRAYER
With these petitions in our hearts, we pray as our brother Jesus taught us: Our Father . . .

SIGN OF PEACE
As a sign of peace, Living God, we offer to you our palms wide open, ready to receive your gift of light and love. May your peace rest on us.

CLOSING PRAYER
God of darkness and light, bless us as we enter this night. We entrust ourselves and our concerns to your merciful love. May our hearts rest confidently in you. We ask this in your holy name. AMEN

WEEK ONE

MONDAY MORNING

✝

Giver of Life, animate our hearts;
inspire us to renew your creation.

PSALM 104:1, 2b-3, 5, 10, 16-22, 35b
℟ The heavens tell the glory of God; all creation sings for joy.

Bless the Lord, O my soul.
   O Lord my God, you are very great. . . .
You stretch out the heavens like a tent,
   you set the beams of your chambers on the waters,
you make the clouds your chariot,
   you ride on the wings of the wind . . .

You set the earth on its foundations,
   so that it shall never be shaken. . . .

You make springs gush forth in the valleys;
   they flow between the hills . . .

The trees of the Lord are watered abundantly,
   the cedars of Lebanon that he planted.

In them the birds build their nests;
   the stork has its home in the fir trees.
The high mountains are for the wild goats;
   the rocks are a refuge for the coneys.
You have made the moon to mark the seasons;
   the sun knows its time for setting.
You make darkness, and it is night,
   when all the animals of the forest come creeping out.
The young lions roar for their prey,
   seeking their food from God.
When the sun rises, they withdraw
   and lie down in their dens. . . .

Bless the Lord, O my soul.
Praise the Lord!

Glory . . .

SCRIPTURE   Proverbs 8:22-31

The Lord created me at the beginning of his work,
   the first of his acts of long ago.
Ages ago I was set up,
   at the first, before the beginning of the earth.
When there were no depths I was brought forth,
   when there were no springs abounding with water.
Before the mountains had been shaped,
   before the hills, I was brought forth—
when he had not yet made earth and fields,
   or the world's first bits of soil.

When he established the heavens, I was there,
   when he drew a circle on the face of the deep,
when he made firm the skies above,
   when he established the fountains of the deep,
when he assigned to the sea its limit,
   so that the waters might not transgress his command,
when he marked out the foundations of the earth,
   then I was beside him, like a master worker;
and I was daily his delight,
   rejoicing before him always,
rejoicing in his inhabited world
   and delighting in the human race.

The word of the Lord.

INTERCESSIONS

Source of Life, the ever-flowing stream of your love flows through all creation. We too are your creatures, called into existence by your loving invitation to life. And so we pray: *Source of Life, may your life flow through us and bear fruit.*

- Rouse in us delight in the beauty of your creation. *We pray to the Lord.*

- Inspire us to be courageous participants in protecting your creation, the work of your hands. *We pray to the Lord.*

- Give us minds eager to study and learn more and more about the natural world. *We pray to the Lord.*

THE LORD'S PRAYER
With these petitions in our hearts, we pray as our brother Jesus taught us: Our Father . . .

SIGN OF PEACE
As a sign of peace, Living God, we offer to you our palms wide open, ready to receive your gift of light and love. May your peace rest on us.

CLOSING PRAYER
Wisdom of God, you were with God as master worker, as creation was born. Bring us also to stand with you in the unfolding of God's ecology. We ask this in Christ's name. AMEN

WEEK ONE

MONDAY EVENING

Giver of Life, animate our hearts;
inspire us to renew your creation.

PSALM 65:1, 5-13
℟ The heavens tell the glory of God; all creation sings for joy.

Praise is due to you,
   O God, in Zion;
and to you shall vows be performed . . .

By awesome deeds you answer us with deliverance,
   O God of our salvation;
you are the hope of all the ends of the earth
   and of the farthest seas.
By your strength you established the mountains;
   you are girded with might.
You silence the roaring of the seas,
   the roaring of their waves,
   the tumult of the peoples.
Those who live at earth's farthest bounds are awed by your signs;
you make the gateways of the morning and the evening shout for joy.

You visit the earth and water it,
  you greatly enrich it;
the river of God is full of water;
  you provide the people with grain,
  for so you have prepared it.
You water its furrows abundantly,
  settling its ridges,
softening it with showers,
  and blessing its growth.
You crown the year with your bounty;
  your wagon tracks overflow with richness.
The pastures of the wilderness overflow,
  the hills gird themselves with joy,
the meadows clothe themselves with flocks,
  the valleys deck themselves with grain,
  they shout and sing together for joy.

Glory . . .

SCRIPTURE   John 1:1-5

In the beginning was the Word, and the Word was with God, and the Word was God. He was in the beginning with God. All things came into being through him, and without him not one thing came into being. What has come into being in him was life, and the life was the light of all people. The light shines in the darkness, and the darkness did not overcome it.

The Gospel of the Lord.

REFLECTION
Where do you experience God's care manifested in creation?

INTERCESSIONS
In the company of Holy Wisdom, you called all that is into being. Open our eyes to the wonder of your work. And so we pray: *Source of Life, may your life flow through us and bear fruit.*

- Inspire us to be eager participants in protecting your creation, the work of your hands. *We pray to the Lord.*
- Enkindle in us love for the human and nonhumans with whom we share our world. *We pray to the Lord.*
- Open our minds to the grandeur of the cosmos. *We pray to the Lord.*

THE LORD'S PRAYER
With these petitions in our hearts, we pray as our brother Jesus taught us: Our Father . . .

SIGN OF PEACE
As a sign of peace, Living God, we offer to you our palms wide open, ready to receive your gift of light and love. May your peace rest on us.

CLOSING PRAYER

God of day and darkness, be with us as we conclude this day. May our rest refresh us and reinvigorate us for our tasks in your service tomorrow. We ask this in Christ's name. AMEN

WEEK ONE

TUESDAY MORNING

✝

Giver of Life, animate our hearts;
inspire us to renew your creation.

PSALM 148:1-4, 7-10, 13
℟ The heavens tell the glory of God; all creation sings for joy.

Praise the Lord!
Praise the Lord from the heavens;
   praise him in the heights!
Praise him, all his angels;
   praise him, all his host!

Praise him, sun and moon;
   praise him, all you shining stars!
Praise him, you highest heavens,
   and you waters above the heavens! . . .

Praise the Lord from the earth,
   you sea monsters and all deeps,
fire and hail, snow and frost,
   stormy wind fulfilling his command!

Mountains and all hills,
   fruit trees and all cedars!
Wild animals and all cattle,
   creeping things and flying birds! . . .

Let them praise the name of the Lord,
   for his name alone is exalted;
   his glory is above earth and heaven.

Glory . . .

SCRIPTURE   Genesis 1:14-18

And God said, "Let there be lights in the dome of the sky to separate the day from the night; and let them be for signs and for seasons and for days and years, and let them be lights in the dome of the sky to give light upon the earth." And it was so. God made the two great lights—the greater light to rule the day and the lesser light to rule the night—and the stars. God set them in the dome of the sky to give light upon the earth, to rule over the day and over the night, and to separate the light from the darkness. And God saw that it was good.

The word of the Lord.

INTERCESSIONS

God of the cosmos, your word alone brought the world into being. We are astonished by your wonderful deeds. And so we pray: *Wellspring of Hope, bestow on us your living wisdom.*

Let There Be Life!   Tuesday Morning

- Rouse us from indifference to the needs of our brothers and sisters. *We pray to the Lord.*
- Biodiversity loss threatens our plant and animal kin. Grant us imagination for effective action. *We pray to the Lord.*
- Grant us the creativity to design a sustainable future for human communities. *We pray to the Lord.*

THE LORD'S PRAYER
With these petitions in our hearts, we pray as our brother Jesus taught us: Our Father . . .

SIGN OF PEACE
As a sign of peace, Living God, we offer to you our palms wide open, ready to receive your gift of light and love. May your peace rest on us.

CLOSING PRAYER
God of creation, prosper our work today that we may make this world a more hospitable common home for all who dwell in it. We ask this in Christ's name. AMEN

WEEK ONE

TUESDAY EVENING

✝

Giver of Life, animate our hearts;
inspire us to renew your creation.

PSALM 104:31-34, 35b
℟ The heavens tell the glory of God; all creation sings for joy.

May the glory of the Lord endure forever;
 may the Lord rejoice in his works—
who looks on the earth and it trembles,
 who touches the mountains and they smoke.

I will sing to the Lord as long as I live;
 I will sing praise to my God while I have being.
May my meditation be pleasing to him,
 for I rejoice in the Lord. . . .

Bless the Lord, O my soul.
Praise the Lord!

Glory . . .

SCRIPTURE   1 John 1:1, 5-7
We declare to you what was from the beginning, what we have heard, what we have seen with our eyes, what we

have looked at and touched with our hands, concerning the word of life. . . . This is the message we have heard from him and proclaim to you, that God is light and in him there is no darkness at all. If we say that we have fellowship with him while we are walking in darkness, we lie and do not do what is true; but if we walk in the light as he himself is in the light, we have fellowship with one another, and the blood of Jesus his Son cleanses us from all sin.

The word of the Lord.

REFLECTION
Put yourself in the place of the writer of the letter that is our scripture this evening. What do you declare that you have heard, seen, and touched with your hands concerning the word of life?

INTERCESSIONS
God of grace and glory, the earth trembles and the mountains smoke when you gaze upon them; human hearts are moved to song. Move us to sing of your wondrous deeds in creation. And so we pray: *Wellspring of Hope, bestow on us your living wisdom.*

- The disruption of water sources caused by climate change threatens the human food supply and animal habitats as well. Help us become better caretakers of aquifers and other natural waters. *We pray to the Lord.*

- God, in you there is light and no darkness at all. Enlighten us, Lord, that we may serve you with glad hearts. *We pray to the Lord.*
- As the darkness of evening enfolds us, help us be mindful of those without safe shelter in the night. *We pray to the Lord.*

THE LORD'S PRAYER
With these petitions in our hearts, we pray as our brother Jesus taught us: Our Father . . .

SIGN OF PEACE
As a sign of peace, Living God, we offer to you our palms wide open, ready to receive your gift of light and love. May your peace rest on us.

CLOSING PRAYER
God of faithful care, we thank you for this day and the people and animals with whom we shared it. Be our refuge this night, and watch over our companions. We ask this in Christ's name. AMEN

WEEK ONE

WEDNESDAY MORNING

✝

Giver of Life, animate our hearts;
inspire us to renew your creation.

PSALM 111:1a, 6-8, 10
℟ The heavens tell the glory of God; all creation sings for joy.

Praise the Lord! . . .
[God] has shown his people the power of his works,
   in giving them the heritage of the nations.
The works of his hands are faithful and just;
   all his precepts are trustworthy.
They are established forever and ever,
   to be performed with faithfulness and uprightness. . . .
The fear of the Lord is the beginning of wisdom;
   all those who practice it have a good understanding.
   His praise endures forever.

Glory . . .

SCRIPTURE   Isaiah 41:17c-20

I the Lord will answer them,
> I the God of Israel will not forsake them.

I will open rivers on the bare heights,
> and fountains in the midst of the valleys;

I will make the wilderness a pool of water,
> and the dry land springs of water.

I will put in the wilderness the cedar,
> the acacia, the myrtle, and the olive;

I will set in the desert the cypress,
> the plane and the pine together,

so that all may see and know,
> all may consider and understand,

that the hand of the Lord has done this,
> the Holy One of Israel has created it.

The word of the Lord.

INTERCESSIONS

Spirit of Life, you brought order and fruitfulness to the world for the flourishing of all. We rejoice in the beauty of creation. And so we pray: *Renewing Spirit, guide us into your new creation.*

- This day, remind us to take time to delight in the lovely sights and sounds and scents of your creation. *We pray to the Lord.*

- The natural world is an intricately woven tapestry. Enlighten us with the interconnection of all creation. *We pray to the Lord.*

- Remind us to be good stewards of the animals and plants in our care. *We pray to the Lord.*

THE LORD'S PRAYER
With these petitions in our hearts, we pray as our brother Jesus taught us: Our Father . . .

SIGN OF PEACE
As a sign of peace, Living God, we offer to you our palms wide open, ready to receive your gift of light and love. May your peace rest on us.

CLOSING PRAYER
God of the acacia and the myrtle, the cedar and the olive, you delight in the rich diversity of life on earth. May we also love the manifold beauty of your creatures, human and nonhuman. We ask this in Christ's name. AMEN

WEEK ONE

WEDNESDAY EVENING

✝

Giver of Life, animate our hearts;
inspire us to renew your creation.

PSALM 50:1-6
℟ The heavens tell the glory of God; all creation sings for joy.

The mighty one, God the Lord,
   speaks and summons the earth
   from the rising of the sun to its setting.
Out of Zion, the perfection of beauty,
   God shines forth.
Our God comes and does not keep silence,
   before him is a devouring fire,
   and a mighty tempest all around him.
He calls to the heavens above
   and to the earth, that he may judge his people:
"Gather to me my faithful ones,
   who made a covenant with me by sacrifice!"
The heavens declare his righteousness,
   for God himself is judge.

Glory . . .

SCRIPTURE   John 17:1-3, 4-8, 13

After Jesus had spoken these words, he looked up to heaven and said, "Father, the hour has come; glorify your Son so that the Son may glorify you, since you have given him authority over all people, to give eternal life to all whom you have given him. . . . I glorified you on earth by finishing the work that you gave me to do. So now, Father, glorify me in your own presence with the glory that I had in your presence before the world existed.

"I have made your name known to those whom you gave me from the world. They were yours, and you gave them to me, and they have kept your word. Now they know that everything you have given me is from you; for the words that you gave to me I have given to them, and they have received them and know in truth that I came from you; and they have believed that you sent me. . . . But now I am coming to you, and I speak these things in the world so that they may have my joy made complete in themselves."

The Gospel of the Lord.

REFLECTION
Jesus glorified God, and asked that God glorify him. What does God's glory mean to you? How do you glorify God?

INTERCESSIONS
God of open love, we learn from the vastness of nature and from the gospel stories about the glories of your creation. You have not left us in the dark, but have made

yourself known in Christ. The Word lived among us to give us life as your sons and daughters. And so we pray: *Renewing Spirit, guide us into your new creation.*

- God of wonder, open to us the witness of nature so that we may see you more clearly. *We pray to the Lord.*
- Holy Spirit, grant us insight that we may be transformed into agents of the gospel. *We pray to the Lord.*
- God of justice, the smallest among us often have the greatest claim to our care. Help us see clearly those we are able to accompany and protect. *We pray to the Lord.*

THE LORD'S PRAYER
With these petitions in our hearts, we pray as our brother Jesus taught us: Our Father . . .

SIGN OF PEACE
As a sign of peace, Living God, we offer to you our palms wide open, ready to receive your gift of light and love. May your peace rest on us.

CLOSING PRAYER
God of glory, wrap us this night in your mantle of peace. We ask this in Christ's name. AMEN

WEEK ONE

THURSDAY MORNING

✝

Giver of Life, animate our hearts;
inspire us to renew your creation.

PSALM 139:7, 13-17
℟ The heavens tell the glory of God; all creation sings for joy.

Where can I go from your spirit?
  Or where can I flee from your presence? . . .

For it was you who formed my inward parts;
  you knit me together in my mother's womb.
I praise you, for I am fearfully and wonderfully made.
  Wonderful are your works;
that I know very well.
  My frame was not hidden from you,
when I was being made in secret,
  intricately woven in the depths of the earth.
Your eyes beheld my unformed substance.

In your book were written
>   all the days that were formed for me,
>   when none of them as yet existed.
> How weighty to me are your thoughts, O God!
>   How vast is the sum of them!

Glory . . .

SCRIPTURE   Isaiah 43:1-3a, 4-7

But now thus says the Lord,
>   he who created you, O Jacob,
>   he who formed you, O Israel:
> Do not fear, for I have redeemed you;
>   I have called you by name, you are mine.
> When you pass through the waters, I will be with you;
>   and through the rivers, they shall not overwhelm you;
> when you walk through fire you shall not be burned,
>   and the flame shall not consume you.
> For I am the Lord your God,
>   the Holy One of Israel, your Savior. . . .
> Because you are precious in my sight,
>   and honored, and I love you,
> I give people in return for you,
>   nations in exchange for your life.
> Do not fear, for I am with you;
>   I will bring your offspring from the east,
>   and from the west I will gather you;

I will say to the north, "Give them up,"
   and to the south, "Do not withhold;
bring my sons from far away
   and my daughters from the end of the earth—
everyone who is called by my name,
   whom I created for my glory,
   whom I formed and made."

The word of the Lord.

INTERCESSIONS
Spirit of faithfulness, your steadfast love is our safety and our salvation. Bring us to imitate your love in solidarity with all creation. And so we pray: *Holy Wisdom, grace us with abundant hope.*

- Open our hearts to recognize your brilliant love in each moment of our days. *We pray to the Lord.*
- Help us appreciate the interconnectedness of all who share this earth. *We pray to the Lord.*
- Love begins with attention. Lead us to attend well to the needs of others. *We pray to the Lord.*

THE LORD'S PRAYER
With these petitions in our hearts, we pray as our brother Jesus taught us: Our Father . . .

SIGN OF PEACE
As a sign of peace, Living God, we offer to you our palms wide open, ready to receive your gift of light and love. May your peace rest on us.

CLOSING PRAYER
Fiery God, be with us this day in our work and in our prayer. May we be a source of hope to all we encounter. We ask this in Christ's name. AMEN.

WEEK ONE

THURSDAY EVENING

Giver of Life, animate our hearts;
inspire us to renew your creation.

PSALM 5:7-8, 11-12
℟ The heavens tell the glory of God; all creation sings for joy.

But I, through the abundance of your steadfast love,
  will enter your house,
I will bow down toward your holy temple
  in awe of you.
Lead me, O Lord, in your righteousness
  because of my enemies;
  make your way straight before me. . . .

[And] let all who take refuge in you rejoice;
  let them ever sing for joy.
Spread your protection over them,
  so that those who love your name may exult in you.
For you bless the righteous, O Lord;
  you cover them with favor as with a shield.

Glory . . .

SCRIPTURE   Luke 12:22-27

He said to his disciples, "Therefore I tell you, do not worry about your life, what you will eat, or about your body, what you will wear. For life is more than food, and the body more than clothing. Consider the ravens: they neither sow nor reap, they have neither storehouse nor barn, and yet God feeds them. Of how much more value are you than the birds! And can any of you by worrying add a single hour to your span of life? If then you are not able to do so small a thing as that, why do you worry about the rest? Consider the lilies, how they grow: they neither toil nor spin; yet I tell you, even Solomon in all his glory was not clothed like one of these.

The Gospel of the Lord.

REFLECTION

What worries would you like to bring to Jesus this day? Will you let him carry them for you?

INTERCESSIONS

God of all hopefulness, the antidote for our worry is hope in you. May the spark of hope be fanned to flame in our hearts this day. And so we pray: *Holy Wisdom, grace us with abundant hope.*

- Worry and anxiety can leave us insensitive to the needs of others. May we let go of worry and embrace compassion. *We pray to the Lord.*

Let There Be Life!

- Spark our imaginations so we may contribute to a more hopeful world. *We pray to the Lord.*
- Let all creation remind us of your tender care. *We pray to the Lord.*

THE LORD'S PRAYER
With these petitions in our hearts, we pray as our brother Jesus taught us: Our Father . . .

SIGN OF PEACE
As a sign of peace, Living God, we offer to you our palms wide open, ready to receive your gift of light and love. May your peace rest on us.

CLOSING PRAYER
Spirit of hope, watch over us this night. May our dreams lead our hearts to trust in you and all your ways. We ask this in Christ's name. AMEN

WEEK ONE

FRIDAY MORNING

✝

Giver of Life, animate our hearts;
inspire us to renew your creation.

PSALM 8:1-6, 9
℟ The heavens tell the glory of God; all creation sings for joy.

O Lord, our Sovereign,
   how majestic is your name in all the earth!

You have set your glory above the heavens.
   Out of the mouths of babes and infants
you have founded a bulwark because of your foes,
   to silence the enemy and the avenger.

When I look at your heavens, the work of your fingers,
   the moon and the stars that you have established;
what are human beings that you are mindful of them,
   mortals that you care for them?

Yet you have made them a little lower than God,
   and crowned them with glory and honor.

You have given them dominion over the works of your hands;
> you have put all things under their feet . . . .

O Lord, our Sovereign,
> how majestic is your name in all the earth!

Glory . . .

SCRIPTURE   Genesis 1:27-31a
So God created humankind in his image,
> in the image of God he created them;
> male and female he created them.

God blessed them, and God said to them, "Be fruitful and multiply, and fill the earth and subdue it; and have dominion over the fish of the sea and over the birds of the air and over every living thing that moves upon the earth." God said, "See, I have given you every plant yielding seed that is upon the face of all the earth, and every tree with seed in its fruit; you shall have them for food. And to every beast of the earth, and to every bird of the air, and to everything that creeps on the earth, everything that has the breath of life, I have given every green plant for food." And it was so. God saw everything that he had made, and indeed, it was very good.

The word of the Lord.

INTERCESSIONS

Creator God, you have made us in your image as part of creation and given us care of your world. May we be faithful to the task for which you made us. And so we pray: *Merciful God, renew your life in us.*

- Everything you made is very good. Grant us the wisdom to cherish your creation. *We pray to the Lord.*

- Too often we abuse creation for shortsighted ends. Help us to see with the eyes of eternity. *We pray to the Lord.*

- Injustice to human communities can force them into ecologically dangerous practices. Make us agents of solidarity and equity in this world. *We pray to the Lord.*

THE LORD'S PRAYER

With these petitions in our hearts, we pray as our brother Jesus taught us: Our Father . . .

SIGN OF PEACE

As a sign of peace, Living God, we offer to you our palms wide open, ready to receive your gift of light and love. May your peace rest on us.

CLOSING PRAYER

What are we that you are mindful of us, O God? Help us to be this day the people whom you need us to be. We ask this in Christ's name. AMEN

WEEK ONE

FRIDAY EVENING

Giver of Life, animate our hearts;
inspire us to renew your creation.

PSALM 66:3a, 4-5, 16-20
℟ The heavens tell the glory of God; all creation sings for joy.

Say to God, "How awesome are your deeds! . . .

All the earth worships you;
  they sing praises to you,
  sing praises to your name."

Come and see what God has done:
  he is awesome in his deeds among mortals. . . .

Come and hear, all you who fear God,
  and I will tell what he has done for me.
I cried aloud to him,
  and he was extolled with my tongue.
If I had cherished iniquity in my heart,
  the Lord would not have listened.
But truly God has listened;
  he has given heed to the words of my prayer.

Blessed be God,
> because he has not rejected my prayer
> or removed his steadfast love from me.

Glory . . .

SCRIPTURE   Romans 8:28-30
We know that all things work together for good for those who love God, who are called according to his purpose. For those whom he foreknew he also predestined to be conformed to the image of his Son, in order that he might be the firstborn within a large family. And those whom he predestined he also called; and those whom he called he also justified; and those whom he justified he also glorified.

The word of the Lord.

REFLECTION
We are conformed to the image of Jesus. In what ways would you like to be a sharper reflection of him?

INTERCESSIONS
The glory of God radiates throughout all creation. Humankind is called to reflect that love for the fulfillment of God's hope for creation. And so we pray: *Merciful God, renew your life in us.*

- Help us to see your glory in the least of created things. *We pray to the Lord.*

- Love is perfected in solidarity. Bring us to solidarity with other human societies and with the natural world. *We pray to the Lord.*
- When we abuse or degrade the natural world, we abuse the glory of God. Give us hearts for justice that we may defend our earth. *We pray to the Lord.*

THE LORD'S PRAYER
With these petitions in our hearts, we pray as our brother Jesus taught us: Our Father . . .

SIGN OF PEACE
As a sign of peace, Living God, we offer to you our palms wide open, ready to receive your gift of light and love. May your peace rest on us.

CLOSING PRAYER
Living God, we thank you for this day. Renew our strength so that we may respond to the needs of your world. We ask this in Christ's name. AMEN

WEEK ONE

SATURDAY MORNING

✝

Giver of Life, animate our hearts;
inspire us to renew your creation.

PSALM 145:1-6, 10, 13b
℞ The heavens tell the glory of God; all creation sings for joy.

I will extol you, my God and King,
  and bless your name forever and ever.
Every day I will bless you,
  and praise your name forever and ever.
Great is the Lord, and greatly to be praised;
  his greatness is unsearchable.

One generation shall laud your works to another,
  and shall declare your mighty acts.
On the glorious splendor of your majesty,
  and on your wondrous works, I will meditate.
The might of your awesome deeds shall be proclaimed,
  and I will declare your greatness. . . .

All your works shall give thanks to you, O Lord,
> and all your faithful shall bless you. . . .

The Lord is faithful in all his words,
> and gracious in all his deeds.

Glory . . .

SCRIPTURE   Isaiah 40:12-14, 18, 21, 25-26
Who has measured the waters in the hollow of his hand
> and marked off the heavens with a span,
enclosed the dust of the earth in a measure,
> and weighed the mountains in scales
> and the hills in a balance?
Who has directed the spirit of the Lord,
> or as his counselor has instructed him?
Whom did he consult for his enlightenment,
> and who taught him the path of justice?
Who taught him knowledge,
> and showed him the way of understanding? . . .

To whom then will you liken God,
> or what likeness compare with him? . . .

Have you not known? Have you not heard?
> Has it not been told you from the beginning?
> Have you not understood from the foundations of
>> the earth? . . .

To whom then will you compare me,
> or who is my equal? says the Holy One.

Lift up your eyes on high and see:
>   Who created these?
He who brings out their host and numbers them,
>   calling them all by name;
because he is great in strength,
>   mighty in power,
>   not one is missing.

The word of the Lord.

INTERCESSIONS

You are infinite in wisdom, O God. Your beauty is beyond our imagining. Bring us into the company of those who rejoice with you. And so we pray: *God of Life, we long to dwell in your new creation.*

- Spirit of justice, inspire us to step in to lead where we are needed to work for justice in our communities. *We pray to the Lord.*
- God of healing, open our eyes to the needs of the sick and suffering. *We pray to the Lord.*
- Generous God, may we be grateful recipients of your grace, and extend kindness and mercy to others in turn. *We pray to the Lord.*

THE LORD'S PRAYER

With these petitions in our hearts, we pray as our brother Jesus taught us: Our Father . . .

SIGN OF PEACE
As a sign of peace, Living God, we offer to you our palms wide open, ready to receive your gift of light and love. May your peace rest on us.

CLOSING PRAYER
Powerful God, be with us today as we work, comfort us when we struggle, and give us strength for the day ahead. We ask this in Christ's name. AMEN

WEEK ONE

SATURDAY EVENING

†

Giver of Life, animate our hearts;
inspire us to renew your creation.

PSALM 148:1-10, 12-14
℟ The heavens tell the glory of God; all creation sings for joy.

Praise the Lord!
Praise the Lord from the heavens;
   praise him in the heights!
Praise him, all his angels;
   praise him, all his host!

Praise him, sun and moon;
   praise him, all you shining stars!
Praise him, you highest heavens,
   and you waters above the heavens!

Let them praise the name of the Lord,
   for he commanded and they were created.
He established them forever and ever;
   he fixed their bounds, which cannot be passed.

Praise the Lord from the earth,
   you sea monsters and all deeps,

fire and hail, snow and frost,
   stormy wind fulfilling his command!

Mountains and all hills,
   fruit trees and all cedars!
Wild animals and all cattle,
   creeping things and flying birds! . . .

Young men and women alike,
   old and young together!

Let them praise the name of the Lord,
   for his name alone is exalted;
   his glory is above earth and heaven.
He has raised up a horn for his people,
   praise for all his faithful,
   for the people of Israel who are close to him.
Praise the Lord!

Glory . . .

SCRIPTURE John 17:22-24

[Jesus said:] "The glory that you have given me I have given them, so that they may be one, as we are one, I in them and you in me, that they may become completely one, so that the world may know that you have sent me and have loved them even as you have loved me. Father, I desire that those also, whom you have given me, may be with me where I am, to see my glory, which you have given me because you loved me before the foundation of the world."

The Gospel of the Lord.

REFLECTION
What would you add to the psalmist's hymn of praise? For what gifts of God are you thankful?

INTERCESSIONS
Creator God, you summon us to life with your Word, and you accompany us in every moment of our lives. And so we pray: *God of Life, we long to dwell in your new creation.*

- Make us people of your peace. *We pray to the Lord.*
- Lead us to joy in your presence. *We pray to the Lord.*
- Fire in us your spirit of justice for all creation. *We pray to the Lord.*

THE LORD'S PRAYER
With these petitions in our hearts, we pray as our brother Jesus taught us: Our Father . . .

SIGN OF PEACE
As a sign of peace, Living God, we offer to you our palms wide open, ready to receive your gift of light and love. May your peace rest on us.

CLOSING PRAYER
Gracious God, we celebrate your creation with all living beings. Keep us faithful in your service, and may our rest this night revive our tired spirits. We ask this in Christ's name. AMEN

Final Thoughts on Celebrating the Gift of Creation

In this week we have been invited to reflect on the beauty and harmony of God's creation. Before there was light, God's Wisdom whispered over the ancient abyss at the cosmic dawn. Even before God commanded light into being, *God is*. The whole of creation is the abode of God, and the Spirit dances in this world. This same Spirit of Life flows in us—in our very blood, in our every breath, and in our yearning for communion. When God summoned humanity into existence, we were welcomed to share the divine project of celebrating, cultivating, and sustaining all that is. We are invited to join in the dance as creation itself glorifies God.

Just as our lives dwell in God, God abides in us. We are created siblings to all that is. In our brother Jesus, we learn how to care for each other. He is our model for walking with mercy and kindness on the earth. With him, we behold the lilies of the field and the birds of the air. In him we feel God's delight in all things. In the ecology of God, we flourish as we cooperate with the Spirit who imbues creation with grace.

Yet humanity over and over again refuses to celebrate creation according to God's design. Instead of cultivating life in its generous abundance, we hoard the earth's riches, taking more than our fair share and despoiling God's gift. Thus begins the alienations that isolate us and harden our hearts. What has gone wrong? Where and how did disharmony interrupt the dance? Why have we so readily strayed from our role as servant-cultivators in the ecology of God? Week Two, *Ruptured Relationships*, will help us reflect and pray about these questions.

WEEK TWO

RUPTURED RELATIONSHIPS

Acknowledging Our Alienation

In Genesis, we hear that God paused after each day's labor to admire the divine handiwork, declaring all to be *good*. There is a natural balance and interdependence within created systems and in the cosmos. The same is true in human relationships, a parallel that Pope Francis details in *Laudato Si'*. "Integral ecology" as defined in the encyclical captures the interconnectedness of human social structures and nature's cycles of growth, flourishing, and decline. Ecclesiasticus's sage words, "For everything there is a season" (Eccl 3:1) express the rhythm of humanity's mutual relationship with God, other human beings, and the natural world: all things in relationship, God alive in all things.

Essential to our relationship with God is the freedom to cooperate and collaborate. God never forces us to love, but beckons us through invitation, affirmation, and inspiration. In our freedom, we can choose to cooperate with God. However, pride, fear, and mistrust lead us to disrupt the order of creation. Humanity's sinful choices spawn disharmony, injustice, greed, and selfishness; they end in strife.

The readings this week summon us to confront and acknowledge our propensity to cultivate estrangements rather than relationships. They highlight the losses that stem from the way our sinful choices alienate others and isolate us. The morning readings trace the familiar story of humanity's fall from relationship with God, removing ourselves from the generosity of God's ecology. Adam and Eve chose to eat the fruit that God had set apart. They became aware of their nakedness and vulnerability. From Cain's jealousy of Abel to the builders' hubris in Babel, people live estranged from one another, and at cross purposes misunderstanding one another. Ruptured relationships easily lead to violence when we replace the practices of giving and receiving in God's ecology with an everyone-for-themselves law of competition and raw power. The pattern of the stories suggests an evolving alienation as the essence of sin: alienation from self, from community, and from God.

The evening readings highlight how alienation wreaks havoc specifically in the human community. Jesus' care for the marginalized, the widows, and the captives offended the community leaders, the priests and Pharisees. His words and actions announced God's favor and generous preference for the poor. The gospel selections share the good news of God's abundant mercy that overcomes all forms of alienation, the most shocking of which is

Ruptured Relationships

Judas's betrayal of Jesus. We are just like people in Jesus' time, when we fail to recognize that God's generosity is God's mercy.

In this week's readings, let us listen intently to the lessons of how we disrupt the ecology of God. Over and over again, we refuse to trust God's generosity, and we choose our own rules over God's way. Jesus reminds us that God seeks us out when we wander, welcomes us back when we return, and trusts us once again to be co-creators nourishing and honoring what God has made.

WEEK TWO

SUNDAY MORNING

✝

Giver of Life, animate our hearts;
inspire us to renew your creation.

PSALM 1:1-6
℟ Rescue us from destruction. Lord, do not delay!

Happy are those
   who do not follow the advice of the wicked,
or take the path that sinners tread,
   or sit in the seat of scoffers;
but their delight is in the law of the Lord,
   and on his law they meditate day and night.
They are like trees
   planted by streams of water,
which yield their fruit in its season,
   and their leaves do not wither.
In all that they do, they prosper.

The wicked are not so,
   but are like chaff that the wind drives away.

Therefore the wicked will not stand in the judgment,
   nor sinners in the congregation of the righteous;
for the Lord watches over the way of the righteous,
   but the way of the wicked will perish.

Glory . . .

SCRIPTURE   Deuteronomy 30:15-19
See, I have set before you today life and prosperity, death and adversity. If you obey the commandments of the Lord your God that I am commanding you today, by loving the Lord your God, walking in his ways, and observing his commandments, decrees, and ordinances, then you shall live and become numerous, and the Lord your God will bless you in the land that you are entering to possess. But if your heart turns away and you do not hear, but are led astray to bow down to other gods and serve them, I declare to you today that you shall perish; you shall not live long in the land that you are crossing the Jordan to enter and possess. I call heaven and earth to witness against you today that I have set before you life and death, blessings and curses. Choose life so that you and your descendants may live[.]

The word of the Lord.

INTERCESSIONS

Gracious God, the psalmist contrasts your people, who follow the law of life, with the "wicked" who reject the call to the beloved community. When we are honest, we recognize ourselves in those who resist caring for others, who seek their own advantage at the cost of others' suffering. And so we pray: *Gracious God, renew our hearts to love your world.*

- Open our eyes to see the ties that bind human suffering to the groaning of our drying, dying world. *We pray to the Lord.*

- Lead us to respond to the urgency of climate change, lest the spark of human desperation flare up into ever more violent conflicts over access to water, space, and food. *We pray to the Lord.*

- Inspire communities to share resources across boundaries and to bear one another's burdens. *We pray to the Lord.*

THE LORD'S PRAYER

With these petitions in our hearts, we pray as our brother Jesus taught us: Our Father . . .

SIGN OF PEACE

As a sign of peace, Living God, we offer to you our bowed heads and contrite hearts, acknowledging our failure to care for creation and one another. May your peace rest on us.

CLOSING PRAYER
May our gracious and loving God forgive us for our selfish fears and teach us how to choose God's law in all we do. We ask this in Christ's name. AMEN

WEEK TWO

SUNDAY EVENING

✝

Giver of Life, animate our hearts;
inspire us to renew your creation.

PSALM 77:2-3, 14-20
℟ Rescue us from destruction. Lord, do not delay!

In the day of my trouble I seek the Lord;
    in the night my hand is stretched out without wearying;
    my soul refuses to be comforted.
I think of God, and I moan;
    I meditate, and my spirit faints. . . .

You are the God who works wonders;
    you have displayed your might among the peoples.
With your strong arm you redeemed your people,
    the descendants of Jacob and Joseph.

When the waters saw you, O God,
    when the waters saw you, they were afraid;
    the very deep trembled.
The clouds poured out water;
    the skies thundered;
    your arrows flashed on every side.

The crash of your thunder was in the whirlwind;
  your lightnings lit up the world;
  the earth trembled and shook.
Your way was through the sea,
  your path, through the mighty waters;
  yet your footprints were unseen.
You led your people like a flock
  by the hand of Moses and Aaron.

Glory . . .

SCRIPTURE   Matthew 7:12-20

[Jesus said:] "In everything do to others as you would have them do to you; for this is the law and the prophets.

"Enter through the narrow gate; for the gate is wide and the road is easy that leads to destruction, and there are many who take it. For the gate is narrow and the road is hard that leads to life, and there are few who find it.

"Beware of false prophets, who come to you in sheep's clothing but inwardly are ravenous wolves. You will know them by their fruits. Are grapes gathered from thorns, or figs from thistles? In the same way, every good tree bears good fruit, but the bad tree bears bad fruit. A good tree cannot bear bad fruit, nor can a bad tree bear good fruit. Every tree that does not bear good fruit is cut down and thrown into the fire. Thus you will know them by their fruits."

The Gospel of the Lord.

REFLECTION
What do your actions (the fruits of your decisions) say about who you are and what you value?

INTERCESSIONS
Loving God, we need only follow your lead and take shelter in your steadfast love to flourish on the land. Even so, we have lost the path that you set before us. And so we pray: *Gracious God, renew our hearts to love your world.*

- Have mercy on us so that we may return to the path of life and your ecology of grace and mercy. *We pray to the Lord.*

- Increase our commitment to climate justice, so that justice roots itself in our words and deeds. *We pray to the Lord.*

- Do not spurn our efforts to reform our lives, but give us grace upon grace to live in your ecology where all are nourished. *We pray to the Lord.*

THE LORD'S PRAYER
With these petitions in our hearts, we pray as our brother Jesus taught us: Our Father . . .

SIGN OF PEACE
As a sign of peace, Living God, we offer to you our bowed heads and contrite hearts, acknowledging our failure to care for creation and one another. May your peace rest on us.

CLOSING PRAYER

May God's grace hold us close as we examine the roots of our alienation. May we have the courage to turn from indifference to kinship and solidarity. We ask this in Christ's name. AMEN

WEEK TWO

MONDAY MORNING

✝

Giver of Life, animate our hearts;
inspire us to renew your creation.

PSALM 141:1-5, 9-10
℟ Rescue us from destruction. Lord, do not delay!

I call upon you, O Lord; come quickly to me;
   give ear to my voice when I call to you.
Let my prayer be counted as incense before you,
   and the lifting up of my hands as an evening sacrifice.
Set a guard over my mouth, O Lord;
   keep watch over the door of my lips.
Do not turn my heart to any evil,
   to busy myself with wicked deeds
in company with those who work iniquity;
   do not let me eat their delicacies.

Let the righteous strike me;
   let the faithful correct me.
Never let the oil of the wicked anoint my head,

Ruptured Relationships   *Monday Morning*

> for my prayer is continually against their wicked
> > deeds. . . .
>
> Keep me from the trap that they have laid for me,
> > and from the snares of evildoers.
> Let the wicked fall into their own nets,
> > while I alone escape.

Glory . . .

SCRIPTURE   Genesis 3:8-13a

They heard the sound of the Lord God walking in the garden at the time of the evening breeze, and the man and his wife hid themselves from the presence of the Lord God among the trees of the garden. But the Lord God called to the man, and said to him, "Where are you?" He said, "I heard the sound of you in the garden, and I was afraid, because I was naked; and I hid myself." He said, "Who told you that you were naked? Have you eaten from the tree of which I commanded you not to eat?" The man said, "The woman whom you gave to be with me, she gave me fruit from the tree, and I ate." Then the Lord God said to the woman, "What is this that you have done?"

The word of the Lord.

INTERCESSIONS

God of justice, we often hide from the consequences of our indifference and selfish choices. To be converted to the ecology of God, we need courage to acknowledge where we have harmed others. And so we pray: *Source of Life, may your life flow through us and bear fruit.*

- Guide us to be steadfast in our witness for climate justice, especially supporting the right of all people to live and thrive. *We pray to the Lord.*
- Tear down the walls we have built around our hearts, and show us the path of full human kinship. *We pray to the Lord.*
- Move us to accept the small and large burdens upon our lifestyle that will make our economy more humane and sustainable. *We pray to the Lord.*

THE LORD'S PRAYER
With these petitions in our hearts, we pray as our brother Jesus taught us: Our Father . . .

SIGN OF PEACE
As a sign of peace, Living God, we offer to you our bowed heads and contrite hearts to acknowledge our failure to care for creation and one another. May your peace rest on us.

CLOSING PRAYER
Gracious God, who receives not just the righteous but also those who need forgiveness, grant us the grace to end alienation in our relationships with others both near and far. We ask this in Christ's name. AMEN

WEEK TWO

MONDAY EVENING

✝

Giver of Life, animate our hearts;
inspire us to renew your creation.

PSALM 143:1-4, 7-8
℟ Rescue us from destruction. Lord, do not delay!

Hear my prayer, O Lord;
> give ear to my supplications in your faithfulness;
> answer me in your righteousness.

Do not enter into judgment with your servant,
> for no one living is righteous before you.

For the enemy has pursued me,
> crushing my life to the ground,
> making me sit in darkness like those long dead.

Therefore my spirit faints within me;
> my heart within me is appalled. . . .

Answer me quickly, O Lord;
> my spirit fails.

Do not hide your face from me,
> or I shall be like those who go down to the Pit. . . .

Let me hear of your steadfast love in the morning,
> for in you I put my trust.

Teach me the way I should go,
> for to you I lift up my soul.

Glory . . .

SCRIPTURE   Luke 11:37-44

While [Jesus] was speaking, a Pharisee invited him to dine with him; so he went in and took his place at the table. The Pharisee was amazed to see that he did not first wash before dinner. Then the Lord said to him, "Now you Pharisees clean the outside of the cup and of the dish, but inside you are full of greed and wickedness. You fools! Did not the one who made the outside make the inside also? So give for alms those things that are within; and see, everything will be clean for you.

"But woe to you Pharisees! For you tithe mint and rue and herbs of all kinds, and neglect justice and the love of God; it is these you ought to have practiced, without neglecting the others. Woe to you Pharisees! For you love to have the seat of honor in the synagogues and to be greeted with respect in the marketplaces. Woe to you! For you are like unmarked graves, and people walk over them without realizing it."

The Gospel of the Lord.

REFLECTION
What is the first step you can take to make your ecological actions consistent with your hope for ecological well-being?

INTERCESSIONS
God of justice, Jesus burned with your justice defending the *anawim* who have always carried the burden of sinful social structures. Only when our society becomes steeped in kinship without borders will all your people thrive. And so we pray: *Source of Life, may your life flow through us and bear fruit.*

- Give us leaders of moral courage, who desire to serve the well-being of the community rather than their own vanity. *We pray to the Lord.*
- Impart in us a deeper desire to conform our actions to our commitments. *We pray to the Lord.*
- Grant us all a greater appreciation of the inseparable bond between climate justice and community flourishing. *We pray to the Lord.*

THE LORD'S PRAYER
With these petitions in our hearts, we pray as our brother Jesus taught us: Our Father . . .

SIGN OF PEACE
As a sign of peace, Living God, we offer to you our bowed heads and contrite hearts, acknowledging our failure to care for creation and one another. May your peace rest on us.

CLOSING PRAYER
May God's justice infuse our hearts and saturate all we do so that our actions make a difference to heal a suffering world. We ask this in Christ's name. AMEN

WEEK TWO

TUESDAY MORNING

✝

Giver of Life, animate our hearts;
inspire us to renew your creation.

PSALM 109:26-31
℟ Rescue us from destruction. Lord, do not delay!

Help me, O Lord my God!
    Save me according to your steadfast love.
Let them know that this is your hand;
    you, O Lord, have done it.
Let them curse, but you will bless.
    Let my assailants be put to shame; may your servant
        be glad.
May my accusers be clothed with dishonor;
    may they be wrapped in their own shame as in a mantle.
With my mouth I will give great thanks to the Lord;
    I will praise him in the midst of the throng.
For he stands at the right hand of the needy,
    to save them from those who would condemn them
        to death.

Glory . . .

SCRIPTURE   Genesis 4:1-9

Now the man knew his wife Eve, and she conceived and bore Cain, saying, "I have produced a man with the help of the Lord." Next she bore his brother Abel. Now Abel was a keeper of sheep, and Cain a tiller of the ground. In the course of time Cain brought to the Lord an offering of the fruit of the ground, and Abel for his part brought of the firstlings of his flock, their fat portions. And the Lord had regard for Abel and his offering, but for Cain and his offering he had no regard. So Cain was very angry, and his countenance fell. The Lord said to Cain, "Why are you angry, and why has your countenance fallen? If you do well, will you not be accepted? And if you do not do well, sin is lurking at the door; its desire is for you, but you must master it."

Cain said to his brother Abel, "Let us go out to the field." And when they were in the field, Cain rose up against his brother Abel, and killed him. Then the Lord said to Cain, "Where is your brother Abel?" He said, "I do not know; am I my brother's keeper?"

The word of the Lord.

INTERCESSIONS

Gracious God, through the story of the first brothers, you warn us about the dangers of pride and ambition. In our actions, solidarity and care too often give way to exploitation and indifference. We need your merciful

Ruptured Relationships   *Tuesday Morning*

love. And so we pray: *Wellspring of Hope, bestow on us your living wisdom.*

- Teach us to weigh generosity as the measure of our worth, rather than possessions and status. *We pray to the Lord.*
- Help us to see the dignity of all your people and the preciousness of all living creatures. *We pray to the Lord.*
- Do not abandon us in the darkness of these turbulent times. *We pray to the Lord.*

THE LORD'S PRAYER
With these petitions in our hearts, we pray as our brother Jesus taught us: Our Father . . .

SIGN OF PEACE
As a sign of peace, Living God, we offer to you our bowed heads and contrite hearts, acknowledging our failure to care for creation and one another. May your peace rest on us.

CLOSING PRAYER
May the graciousness of God fill our hearts and restore our relationships so that kinship becomes a reality in our day. May we become keepers of one another's well-being. We ask this in Christ's name. AMEN

WEEK TWO

TUESDAY EVENING

✝

Giver of Life, animate our hearts;
inspire us to renew your creation.

PSALM 139:1-7, 23-24
℟ Rescue us from destruction. Lord, do not delay!

O Lord, you have searched me and known me.
You know when I sit down and when I rise up;
 you discern my thoughts from far away.
You search out my path and my lying down,
 and are acquainted with all my ways.
Even before a word is on my tongue,
 O Lord, you know it completely.
You hem me in, behind and before,
 and lay your hand upon me.
Such knowledge is too wonderful for me;
 it is so high that I cannot attain it.

Where can I go from your spirit?
 Or where from can I flee from your presence? . . .

Search me, O God, and know my heart;
 test me and know my thoughts.

Ruptured Relationships   *Tuesday Evening*

See if there is any wicked way in me,
    and lead me in the way everlasting.

Glory . . .

SCRIPTURE   Luke 10:29-37

[He] asked Jesus, "And who is my neighbor?" Jesus replied, "A man was going down from Jerusalem to Jericho, and fell into the hands of robbers, who stripped him, beat him, and went away, leaving him half dead. Now by chance a priest was going down that road; and when he saw him, he passed by on the other side. So likewise a Levite, when he came to the place and saw him, passed by on the other side. But a Samaritan while traveling came near him; and when he saw him, he was moved with pity. He went to him and bandaged his wounds, having poured oil and wine on them. Then he put him on his own animal, brought him to an inn, and took care of him. The next day he took out two denarii, gave them to the innkeeper, and said, 'Take care of him; and when I come back, I will repay you whatever more you spend.' Which of these three, do you think, was a neighbor to the man who fell into the hands of the robbers?" He said, "The one who showed him mercy." Jesus said to him, "Go and do likewise."

The Gospel of the Lord.

REFLECTION
Who is your neighbor? What has that cost you?

INTERCESSIONS
Gracious God, Jesus shows us that there are no boundaries to your love. Yet we struggle to live in the ecology of gift that you are teaching us. And so we pray: *Wellspring of Hope, bestow on us your living wisdom.*

- Humble us to receive the ministries of others so that their gift may teach us generosity. *We pray to the Lord.*
- Ignite us with the conviction and courage of the good Samaritan to "go and do likewise" for our neighbors. *We pray to the Lord.*
- Examine our lives and show us where we can grow in neighborly love for our planet and your people. *We pray to the Lord.*

THE LORD'S PRAYER
With these petitions in our hearts, we pray as our brother Jesus taught us: Our Father . . .

SIGN OF PEACE
As a sign of peace, Living God, we offer to you our bowed heads and contrite hearts, acknowledging our failure to care for creation and one another. May your peace rest on us.

CLOSING PRAYER
May God's mercy heal our ruptured relationships today and all days, until all people welcome one another as neighbors and kin. We ask this in Christ's name. AMEN

WEEK TWO

WEDNESDAY MORNING

✝

Giver of Life, animate our hearts;
inspire us to renew your creation.

PSALM 42:1-3, 5b-8
℟ Rescue us from destruction. Lord, do not delay!

As a deer longs for flowing streams,
 so my soul longs for you, O God.
My soul thirsts for God,
 for the living God.
When shall I come and behold
 the face of God?
My tears have been my food
 day and night,
while people say to me continually,
 "Where is your God?" . . .

Hope in God; for I shall again praise him,
 my help and my God.
My soul is cast down within me;
 therefore I remember you

from the land of Jordan and of Hermon,
   from Mount Mizar.
Deep calls to deep
   at the thunder of your cataracts;
all your waves and your billows
   have gone over me.
By day the Lord commands his steadfast love,
   and at night his song is with me,
   a prayer to the God of my life.

Glory . . .

SCRIPTURE   Genesis 6:12-14, 17-19, 21-22

And God saw that the earth was corrupt; for all flesh had corrupted its ways upon the earth. And God said to Noah, "I have determined to make an end of all flesh, for the earth is filled with violence because of them; now I am going to destroy them along with the earth. Make yourself an ark of cypress wood; make rooms in the ark, and cover it inside and out with pitch. . . . For my part, I am going to bring a flood of waters on the earth, to destroy from under heaven all flesh in which is the breath of life; everything that is on the earth shall die. But I will establish my covenant with you; and you shall come into the ark, you, your sons, your wife, and your sons' wives with you. And of every living thing, of all flesh, you shall bring two of every kind into the ark, to keep them alive with you; they shall be male and female. . . . Also take with you every kind of food that is eaten, and store it up;

and it shall serve as food for you and for them." Noah did this; he did all that God commanded him.

The word of the Lord.

INTERCESSIONS
Compassionate God, you sent the devastating flood in Noah's day because the people had tainted and disrupted your ecology with greed and violence. In our day, human actions have again tainted the world's ecology and all our relationships. Do not let us perish, but save us through your steadfast love. And so we pray: *Renewing Spirit, guide us into your new creation.*

- Hasten the coming of the new covenant of shared abundance, which you promised long ago to your people. *We pray to the Lord.*
- Lift up our souls and give us hope that our world and all its people may be saved from environmental destruction. *We pray to the Lord.*
- Reveal to us the structures of our economy that violate the lives and dignity of the poor and the youth. *We pray to the Lord.*

THE LORD'S PRAYER
With these petitions in our hearts, we pray as our brother Jesus taught us: Our Father . . .

SIGN OF PEACE
As a sign of peace, Living God, we offer to you our bowed heads and contrite hearts, acknowledging our failure to care for creation and one another. May your peace rest on us.

CLOSING PRAYER
May the God of mercy bless the work of our hands today. May God bring justice and plenty into the lives of people near and far. We ask this in Christ's name. AMEN

WEEK TWO

WEDNESDAY EVENING

✝

Giver of Life, animate our hearts;
inspire us to renew your creation.

PSALM 43:1-5
℟ Rescue us from destruction. Lord, do not delay!

Vindicate me, O God, and defend my cause
   against an ungodly people;
from those who are deceitful and unjust
   deliver me!
For you are the God in whom I take refuge;
   why have you cast me off?
Why must I walk about mournfully
   because of the oppression of the enemy?

O send out your light and your truth;
   let them lead me;
let them bring me to your holy hill
   and to your dwelling.
Then I will go to the altar of God,
   to God my exceeding joy;
and I will praise you with the harp,
   O God, my God.

Ruptured Relationships   *Wednesday Evening*

Why are you cast down, O my soul,
   and why are you disquieted within me?
Hope in God; for I shall again praise him,
   my help and my God.

Glory . . .

SCRIPTURE   Luke 8:22-25

One day he got into a boat with his disciples, and he said to them, "Let us go across to the other side of the lake." So they put out, and while they were sailing he fell asleep. A windstorm swept down on the lake, and the boat was filling with water, and they were in danger. They went to him and woke him up, shouting, "Master, Master, we are perishing!" And he woke up and rebuked the wind and the raging waves; they ceased, and there was a calm. He said to them, "Where is your faith?" They were afraid and amazed, and said to one another, "Who then is this, that he commands even the winds and the water, and they obey him?"

The Gospel of the Lord.

REFLECTION

Can you imagine a saving miracle today to reestablish a healthy planet? Will you pray to Christ for this?

INTERCESSIONS

Compassionate God, like Jesus' disciples, we only turn to you when we feel ourselves on the verge of destruction, only when the ruptures of our lives threaten to swallow us. And yet your compassion seems endless and your steadfast love inexhaustible. And so we pray: *Renewing Spirit, guide us into your new creation.*

- Seed within us a desire to rededicate ourselves to working for the healing of our planet and the renewal of all life. *We pray to the Lord.*
- Enkindle within us a renewed commitment to attend faithfully to all that you have created. *We pray to the Lord.*
- Fill us with your compassion and love so that we will be drawn to care for those who have been harmed by our careless approach to the earth's health. *We pray to the Lord.*

THE LORD'S PRAYER
With these petitions in our hearts, we pray as our brother Jesus taught us: Our Father . . .

SIGN OF PEACE
As a sign of peace, Living God, we offer to you our bowed heads and contrite hearts, acknowledging our failure to care for creation and one another. May your peace rest on us.

CLOSING PRAYER
May the God of wisdom enkindle a renewed spirit in our hearts today. May we become guardians of the earth and follow Jesus in his care for those who dwell here. We ask this in Christ's name. AMEN

WEEK TWO

THURSDAY MORNING

✝

Giver of Life, animate our hearts;
inspire us to renew your creation.

PSALM 79:1-5, 8-9, 13
℟ Rescue us from destruction. Lord, do not delay!

O God, the nations have come into your inheritance;
   they have defiled your holy temple;
   they have laid Jerusalem in ruins.
They have given the bodies of your servants
   to the birds of the air for food,
   the flesh of your faithful to the wild animals of the earth.
They have poured out their blood like water
   all around Jerusalem,
   and there was no one to bury them.
We have become a taunt to our neighbors,
   mocked and derided by those around us.

How long, O Lord? Will you be angry forever?
   Will your jealous wrath burn like fire? . . .

Do not remember against us the iniquities of our ancestors;
>   let your compassion come speedily to meet us,
>   for we are brought very low.
Help us, O God of our salvation,
>   for the glory of your name;
> deliver us, and forgive our sins,
>   for your name's sake. . . .

Then we your people, the flock of your pasture,
>   will give thanks to you forever;
>   from generation to generation we will recount your
>   praise.

Glory . . .

SCRIPTURE   Genesis 11:4-8
Then they said, "Come, let us build ourselves a city, and a tower with its top in the heavens, and let us make a name for ourselves; otherwise we shall be scattered abroad upon the face of the whole earth." The Lord came down to see the city and the tower, which mortals had built. And the Lord said, "Look, they are one people, and they have all one language; and this is only the beginning of what they will do; nothing that they propose to do will now be impossible for them. Come, let us go down, and confuse their language there, so that they will not understand one another's speech." So the Lord scattered them abroad from there over the face of all the earth, and they left off building the city.

The word of the Lord.

INTERCESSIONS
Holy Creator, we are so often blind to the groaning of creation and insensitive to the suffering of other people. Then, when we become aware, we despair of healing and rebirth. And so we pray: *Holy Wisdom, grace us with abundant hope.*

- Grant us forgiveness for the times we failed to show empathy, and nurture hope to those most in need. *We pray to the Lord.*

- Summon our attention to those cries welling up from all forms of life on this earth threatened by human indifference and ignorance. *We pray to the Lord.*

- Enable us to grasp that even the small gestures we make to live more cooperatively with all life contribute to the renewal of your creation. *We pray to the Lord.*

THE LORD'S PRAYER
With these petitions in our hearts, we pray as our brother Jesus taught us: Our Father . . .

SIGN OF PEACE
As a sign of peace, Living God, we offer to you our bowed heads and contrite hearts, acknowledging our failure to care for creation and one another. May your peace rest on us.

CLOSING PRAYER

May the Creator and Ruler of the universe, who entrusted the world to us as a gift to cultivate and develop, help us to care for the earth and for its people. We ask this in Christ's name. AMEN

WEEK TWO

THURSDAY EVENING

✝

Giver of Life, animate our hearts;
inspire us to renew your creation.

PSALM 39:4-11
℟ Rescue us from destruction. Lord, do not delay!

"Lord, let me know my end,
 and what is the measure of my days;
 let me know how fleeting my life is.
You have made my days a few handbreadths,
 and my lifetime is as nothing in your sight.
Surely everyone stands as a mere breath.
 Surely everyone goes about like a shadow.
Surely for nothing they are in turmoil;
 they heap up, and do not know who will gather.

"And now, O Lord, what do I wait for?
 My hope is in you.
Deliver me from all my transgressions.
 Do not make me the scorn of the fool.
I am silent; I do not open my mouth,
 for it is you who have done it.

Remove your stroke from me;
  I am worn down by the blows of your hand.

"You chastise mortals
  in punishment for sin,
consuming like a moth what is dear to them;
  surely everyone is a mere breath.

Glory . . .

SCRIPTURE   Luke 4:17b-19, 21-22, 24-26, 28-30

He unrolled the scroll and found the place where it was written:

"The Spirit of the Lord is upon me,
  because he has anointed me
    to bring good news to the poor.
He has sent me to proclaim release to the captives
  and recovery of sight to the blind,
    to let the oppressed go free,
to proclaim the year of the Lord's favor."

And he rolled up the scroll, gave it back to the attendant, and sat down. The eyes of all in the synagogue were fixed on him. Then he began to say to them, "Today this scripture has been fulfilled in your hearing." All spoke well of him and were amazed at the gracious words that came from his mouth. They said, "Is not this Joseph's son?" . . . And he said, "Truly I tell you, no prophet is accepted in the prophet's hometown. But the truth is, there were many widows in Israel in the time of Elijah, when the heaven was shut up three years and six months, and there was a severe famine over all the land; yet Elijah was sent to none of them except to a widow at Zarephath in Sidon. . . . When they heard this, all in the synagogue were filled with rage. They got up, drove him out of the town, and led him to the brow of the hill on which their town was built, so that they might hurl him off the cliff. But he passed through the midst of them and went on his way.

The Gospel of the Lord.

REFLECTION
When in your life have you experienced the power of compassion?

INTERCESSIONS
Gracious God, you gave us your Son who lived among the people and revealed your love to all. Help us to imitate Christ's abundant love for the human family. And so we pray: *Holy Wisdom, grace us with abundant hope.*

- Grant us the ongoing awareness that we are connected to all our brothers and sisters around the world. *We pray to the Lord.*

- Stir us to act on behalf of those most impacted by environmental devastation. *We pray to the Lord.*

- Teach us to live in right relationship with you, with each other, and with all of creation. *We pray to the Lord.*

THE LORD'S PRAYER
With these petitions in our hearts, we pray as our brother Jesus taught us: Our Father . . .

SIGN OF PEACE
As a sign of peace, Living God, we offer to you our bowed heads and contrite hearts, acknowledging our failure to care for creation and one another. May your peace rest on us.

CLOSING PRAYER
May the God of gracious love, who bestows upon us the constancy of divine care, summon us to act as channels of that love toward all of creation. We ask this in Christ's name. AMEN

WEEK TWO

FRIDAY MORNING

✝

Giver of Life, animate our hearts;
inspire us to renew your creation.

PSALM 51:1-4
℟ Rescue us from destruction. Lord, do not delay!

Have mercy on me, O God,
   according to your steadfast love;
according to your abundant mercy
   blot out my transgressions.
Wash me thoroughly from my iniquity,
   and cleanse me from my sin.

For I know my transgressions,
   and my sin is ever before me.
Against you, you alone, have I sinned,
   and done what is evil in your sight,
so that you are justified in your sentence
   and blameless when you pass judgment.

Glory . . .

SCRIPTURE Numbers 20:2-8, 21:4-5

Now there was no water for the congregation; so they gathered together against Moses and against Aaron. The people quarreled with Moses and said, "Would that we had died when our kindred died before the Lord! Why have you brought the assembly of the Lord into this wilderness for us and our livestock to die here? Why have you brought us up out of Egypt, to bring us to this wretched place? It is no place for grain, or figs, or vines, or pomegranates; and there is no water to drink." Then Moses and Aaron went away from the assembly to the entrance of the tent of meeting; they fell on their faces, and the glory of the Lord appeared to them. The Lord spoke to Moses, saying: "Take the staff, and assemble the congregation, you and your brother Aaron, and command the rock before their eyes to yield its water. Thus you shall bring water out of the rock for them; thus you shall provide drink for the congregation and their livestock.". . .

From Mount Hor they set out by the way to the Red Sea, to go around the land of Edom; but the people became impatient on the way. The people spoke against God and against Moses, "Why have you brought us up out of Egypt to die in the wilderness? For there is no food and no water, and we detest this miserable food."

The word of the Lord.

Ruptured Relationships   *Friday Morning*

INTERCESSIONS

Divine Wisdom, pour out your Spirit upon us that we may foster all life in all its forms and beauty. And so we pray: *Merciful God, renew your life in us.*

- Enable us to recognize our shortsightedness and imprudent priorities regarding our use and abuse of the earth's resources. *We pray to the Lord.*
- Help us turn from selfish overconsumption of the earth's gifts that were meant for all. *We pray to the Lord.*
- Chastise our hearts to offer a true confession for all the ways we have wasted and desecrated your creation. *We pray to the Lord.*

THE LORD'S PRAYER

With these petitions in our hearts, we pray as our brother Jesus taught us: Our Father . . .

SIGN OF PEACE

As a sign of peace, Living God, we offer to you our bowed heads and contrite hearts, acknowledging our failure to care for creation and one another. May your peace rest on us.

CLOSING PRAYER

May God bring justice and plenty into the lives of people near and far. We ask this in Christ's name. AMEN

WEEK TWO

FRIDAY EVENING

✝

Giver of Life, animate our hearts;
inspire us to renew your creation.

PSALM 51:10-12, 15-19
℟ Rescue us from destruction. Lord, do not delay!

Create in me a clean heart, O God,
    and put a new and right spirit within me.
Do not cast me away from your presence,
    and do not take your holy spirit from me.
Restore to me the joy of your salvation,
    and sustain in me a willing spirit. . . .

O Lord, open my lips,
    and my mouth will declare your praise.
For you have no delight in sacrifice;
    if I were to give a burnt offering, you would not be pleased.
The sacrifice acceptable to God is a broken spirit;
    a broken and contrite heart, O God, you will not despise.

Do good to Zion in your good pleasure;
    rebuild the walls of Jerusalem,

then you will delight in right sacrifices,
> in burnt offerings and whole burnt offerings;
> then bulls will be offered on your altar.

Glory . . .

SCRIPTURE   John 13:21-38

After saying this Jesus was troubled in spirit, and declared, "Very truly, I tell you, one of you will betray me." The disciples looked at one another, uncertain of whom he was speaking. One of his disciples—the one whom Jesus loved—was reclining next to him; Simon Peter therefore motioned to him to ask Jesus of whom he was speaking. So while reclining next to Jesus, he asked him, "Lord, who is it?" Jesus answered, "It is the one to whom I give this piece of bread when I have dipped it in the dish." So when he had dipped the piece of bread, he gave it to Judas son of Simon Iscariot. After he received the piece of bread, Satan entered into him. Jesus said to him, "Do quickly what you are going to do." Now no one at the table knew why he said this to him. Some thought that, because Judas had the common purse, Jesus was telling him, "Buy what we need for the festival"; or, that he should give something to the poor. So, after receiving the piece of bread, he immediately went out. And it was night.

When he had gone out, Jesus said, "Now the Son of Man has been glorified, and God has been glorified in him. If God has been glorified in him, God will also glorify him in himself and will glorify him at once. Little children, I am with you only a little longer. You will look for me; and as I said to the Jews so now I say to you, 'Where I am going, you cannot come.' I give you a new commandment, that you love one another. Just as I have loved you, you also should love one another. By this everyone will know that you are my disciples, if you have love for one another."

Simon Peter said to him, "Lord, where are you going?" Jesus answered, "Where I am going, you cannot follow me now; but you will follow afterward." Peter said to him, "Lord, why can I not follow you now? I will lay down my life for you." Jesus answered, "Will you lay down your life for me? Very truly, I tell you, before the cock crows, you will have denied me three times."

The Gospel of the Lord.

REFLECTION
In what ways are my spiritual practices connected or not connected to how I live in God's creation?

INTERCESSIONS
Holy Spirit, fill us with the awareness that all life on earth deserves protection and care. And so we pray: *Merciful God, renew your life in us.*

- May the prophetic spirit of Jesus inspire our leaders to hear the cries of those most affected by climate change. *We pray to the Lord.*

Ruptured Relationships   *Friday Evening*

- Deepen our gratitude for all that you have made. *We pray to the Lord.*
- Give us the courage to act urgently and wisely so that our common home may be healed and restored. *We pray to the Lord.*

THE LORD'S PRAYER
With these petitions in our hearts, we pray as our brother Jesus taught us: Our Father . . .

SIGN OF PEACE
As a sign of peace, Living God, we offer to you our bowed heads and contrite hearts, acknowledging our failure to care for creation and one another. May your peace rest on us.

CLOSING PRAYER
May the God, the giver of all life, renew a lively determination in each of us to nurture and care for all life on our planet. We ask this in Christ's name. AMEN

WEEK TWO

SATURDAY MORNING

✝

Giver of Life, animate our hearts;
inspire us to renew your creation.

PSALM 31:1-2, 9-10, 19, 21, 24
℟ Rescue us from destruction. Lord, do not delay!

In you, O Lord, I seek refuge;
> do not let me ever be put to shame;
> in your righteousness deliver me.
Incline your ear to me;
> rescue me speedily.
Be a rock of refuge for me,
> a strong fortress to save me. . . .

Be gracious to me, O Lord, for I am in distress;
> my eye wastes away from grief,
> my soul and body also.
For my life is spent with sorrow,
> and my years with sighing;
my strength fails because of my misery,
> and my bones waste away. . . .

O how abundant is your goodness
   that you have laid up for those who fear you,
and accomplished for those who take refuge in you,
   in the sight of everyone! . . .

Blessed be the Lord,
   for he has wondrously shown his steadfast love to me
   when I was beset as a city under siege. . . .

Be strong, and let your heart take courage,
   all you who wait for the Lord.

Glory . . .

SCRIPTURE   Deuteronomy 30:4, 6, 8-10

Even if you are exiled to the ends of the world, from there the Lord your God will gather you, and from there he will bring you back. . . . Moreover, the Lord your God will circumcise your heart and the heart of your descendants, so that you will love the Lord your God with all your heart and with all your soul, in order that you may live. . . . Then you shall again obey the Lord, observing all his commandments that I am commanding you today, and the Lord your God will make you abundantly prosperous in all your undertakings, in the fruit of your body, in the fruit of your livestock, and in the fruit of your soil. For the Lord will again take delight in prospering you, just as he delighted in prospering your ancestors, when you obey the Lord your God by observing his commandments and decrees that are written in this book of the law, because you turn to the Lord your God with all your heart and with all your soul.

The word of the Lord.

INTERCESSIONS

Source of Life, we long to dwell in your new creation and recognize that our care of it makes us servant-cultivators with you. And so we pray: *God of Life, we long to dwell in your new creation.*

- Enable us to view this earth with reverence and all its life as a sanctuary of your presence. *We pray to the Lord.*
- Give us the grace to grasp that we are intimately joined to all forms of life on this earth. *We pray to the Lord.*
- Strengthen our commitment to work to sow beauty and to protest life against forces that destroy it. *We pray to the Lord.*

THE LORD'S PRAYER

With these petitions in our hearts, we pray as our brother Jesus taught us: Our Father . . .

SIGN OF PEACE

As a sign of peace, Living God, we offer to you our bowed heads and contrite hearts, acknowledging our failure to care for creation and one another. May your peace rest on us.

CLOSING PRAYER

May God, who is gracious and good, enable us to recognize how profoundly we are connected to one another in this marvelous creation. We ask this in Christ's name.
AMEN

WEEK TWO

SATURDAY EVENING

✝

Giver of Life, animate our hearts;
inspire us to renew your creation.

PSALM 57:1-9
℟ Rescue us from destruction. Lord, do not delay!

Be merciful to me, O God, be merciful to me,
  for in you my soul takes refuge;
in the shadow of your wings I will take refuge,
  until the destroying storms pass by.
I cry to God Most High,
  to God who fulfills his purpose for me.
He will send from heaven and save me,
  he will put to shame those who trample on me.
God will send forth his steadfast love and his faithfulness.

I lie down among lions
  that greedily devour human prey;
their teeth are spears and arrows,
  their tongues sharp swords.

Be exalted, O God, above the heavens.
  Let your glory be over all the earth.

Ruptured Relationships   *Saturday Evening*

They set a net for my steps;
   my soul was bowed down.
They dug a pit in my path,
   but they have fallen into it themselves.
My heart is steadfast, O God,
   my heart is steadfast,
I will sing and make melody.
   Awake, my soul!
Awake, O harp and lyre!
   I will awake the dawn.
I will give thanks to you, O Lord, among the peoples;
   I will sing praises to you among the nations.

Glory . . .

SCRIPTURE   Mark 2:13-17

Jesus went out again beside the sea; the whole crowd gathered around him, and he taught them. As he was walking along, he saw Levi son of Alphaeus sitting at the tax booth, and he said to him, "Follow me." And he got up and followed him.

   And as he sat at dinner in Levi's house, many tax collectors and sinners were also sitting with Jesus and his disciples—for there were many who followed him. When the scribes of the Pharisees saw that he was eating with sinners and tax collectors, they said to his disciples, "Why does he eat with tax collectors and sinners?" When Jesus heard this, he said to them, "Those who are well have no need of a physician, but those who are sick; I have come to call not the righteous but sinners."

The Gospel of the Lord.

REFLECTION
Imagine you are eating with Jesus at Levi's house. What is the mood of the guests?

INTERCESSIONS
Source of Life, we long to dwell in your new creation. Encourage us with your grace to continue the struggle for climate justice and human flourishing. And so we pray: *God of Life, we long to dwell in your new creation.*

- Forgive the ways that we have contributed to needless suffering of others and harmed other forms of life. *We pray to the Lord.*
- Heal our vision so as to overcome the veil that blinds us to the ways we ignore injustices in our world. *We pray to the Lord.*
- Infuse our awareness with a sense of awe and gratitude as we behold your gifts that support our life each day. *We pray to the Lord.*

THE LORD'S PRAYER
With these petitions in our hearts, we pray as our brother Jesus taught us: Our Father . . .

SIGN OF PEACE
As a sign of peace, Living God, we offer to you our bowed heads and contrite hearts, acknowledging our failure to care for creation and one another. May your peace rest on us.

CLOSING PRAYER
May the God who continues to summon us to join in the work of creation stir us from our indifference. May we recognize in Jesus' friendship with sinners not a reprimand but a graced promise of healing. We ask this in Christ's name. AMEN

Final Thoughts about Ruptured Relationships

During this week we have pondered the wreckage of alienation—how our estrangement from God echoes in disrupted human society and in the way we abuse the natural world. The alienations we have wrought are, ultimately, self-destructive. Ruptured relationships destroy our common home and shatter the community, especially the lives of vulnerable people on the margins. We find ourselves separated from the natural world as well, because we refuse to share God's joy in creation.

Human relationships of abuse and injustice can be made right, but only through ongoing care and assiduous work. Our labors can support creation's rejuvenation. If we let the inner generativity of the ecology of God reassert itself, we might again see creation as it flourished to God's primal delight. But our desire and labor are not enough; we need redemption.

Our *metanoia* and return to God's ecology begin when we recognize the rupture of our choices. The redemption of humanity and all creation requires God-with-us, Jesus Emmanuel, to restore all things into right relationship with God. In Christ, God's invitation to restore caring relationships remains always open to us. Through the Spirit's grace, our deafness and blindness are healed; our ears and eyes are opened. We must be honest enough to acknowledge how we have strayed from our place in God's design.

Still we know that God's redeeming outreach precedes our conversion. This invitation is the heart of Week Three, *Healing Creation*. To accept Christ's salvation, we listen and learn what God's ecology means. We turn back to God, accepting ourselves in solidarity and kinship and the possibility of cultivating a glorious creation, where love saturates the cosmos. In Jesus we experience the good news of life in the ecology of God.

WEEK THREE

HEALING CREATION

Accepting Christ's Salvation

God is present in and to all creation, including flawed and fallible humanity. The readings this week remind us of God's inexhaustible care as God renews the promise of salvation over and over again. Salvation is not a moment—it is a process of reconnection as we strive to live into the divine invitation to intimacy and healing.

The readings show us that Jesus saves us as he rebalances our relationships with one another, between God and us, and, ultimately, among all creatures. The morning readings highlight how healing broken connections yields abundance and plenty. When we turn our faces to God, we leave the edges of fields unharvested for the poor to glean the fruits of the earth, assuring that the abundance of the fields is fully shared. A hungry woman miraculously has enough when she shares her last oil and flour with the prophet Elijah. God waters the burning desert into a green oasis. Dry bones are raised again to new life. People are promised the coming of a servant of God who brings justice to the world. Perhaps most startlingly, we hear that we have God's law of generosity and mercy written on our hearts: we are created to be agents as well as recipients of God's salvation. We have been entrusted with the ecology of God to save and heal the world, in communion with Jesus Christ.

Jesus' very name is salvation: in Hebrew, *Yehoshua* (sometimes shortened to *Yeshua*) means "God will save." *Salvation* is another term for our return to the ecology of God, when we live in kinship and solidarity. Our evening readings highlight Jesus' actions and teachings as he reveals that divine ecosystem. We learn that the whole of the law is a command to love God and neighbor when we see Jesus enact that command by teaching and feeding a hungry crowd. As in the Hebrew Bible, the presence of God becomes manifest through amazing signs, healing the sick and bestowing life to a child who has died. Jesus shows us the way to cultivate life in the ecology of God. He calls us to be servants of others and to share in the Eucharist. Redemption includes the invitation to embody Christ on earth.

As we pray through this week, we notice the movement from distance to intimacy and from harm to healing. In God's ecology, divine life renews creation in gift after gift. We can recognize that our lives are essential to rebuilding God's ecology. As we turn back to God, the healing and restoration of bodies and relationships becomes possible. When we live in Christ, the disrupted harmony of creation can be put right again. Christ's eternally new law is the law of love of God and neighbor, encompassing all life that the Word of God animates. Fed in body and soul at the table of the Eucharist, we are called forth to labor for the good of all that God has created.

WEEK THREE

SUNDAY MORNING

☦

Giver of Life, animate our hearts;
inspire us to renew your creation.

PSALM 62:1-2, 5-7
℟ In this season of your mercy, O Lord, call us back to life.

For God alone my soul waits in silence;
   from him comes my salvation.
He alone is my rock and my salvation, my fortress;
   I shall never be shaken. . . .

For God alone my soul waits in silence,
   for my hope is from him.
He alone is my rock and my salvation,
   my fortress; I shall not be shaken.
On God rests my deliverance and my honor;
   my mighty rock, my refuge is in God.

Glory . . .

SCRIPTURE   Jeremiah 15:19-21

Therefore thus says the Lord:
If you turn back, I will take you back,
   and you shall stand before me.
If you utter what is precious, and not what is worthless,
   you shall serve as my mouth.
It is they who will turn to you,
   not you who will turn to them.
And I will make you to this people
   a fortified wall of bronze;
they will fight against you,
   but they shall not prevail over you,
for I am with you
   to save you and deliver you,
      says the Lord.
I will deliver you out of the hand of the wicked,
   and redeem you from the grasp of the ruthless.

The word of the Lord.

INTERCESSIONS

Loving God, you call to us with promises of forgiveness and reconciliation. Help us to trust that you will take us back and redeem us through Christ's saving love. And so we pray: *Gracious God, renew our hearts to love your world.*

- Strengthen our hearts to champion a living wage and a healthy environment for all people. *We pray to the Lord.*
- By the work of our willing hands and converted hearts, heal the damage we have wreaked upon our Mother Earth. *We pray to the Lord.*
- Grant us patience and perseverance as we rebuild the communities unjustly suffering from climate change. *We pray to the Lord.*

THE LORD'S PRAYER
With these petitions in our hearts, we pray as our brother Jesus taught us: Our Father . . .

SIGN OF PEACE
As a sign of peace, Living God, we offer you our open arms and hopeful faces to welcome your saving grace. May your peace rest on us.

CLOSING BLESSING
May we trust in forgiveness through Jesus' redemption and the divine promise of life everlasting. We ask this in Christ's name. AMEN

WEEK THREE

SUNDAY EVENING

Giver of Life, animate our hearts;
inspire us to renew your creation.

PSALM 62:8, 11-12

℟ In this season of your mercy, O Lord, call us back to life.

Trust in him at all times, O people;
   pour out your heart before him;
   God is a refuge for us. . . .

Once God has spoken;
   twice have I heard this:
that power belongs to God,
   and steadfast love belongs to you, O Lord.
For you repay to all
   according to their work.

Glory . . .

SCRIPTURE   Luke 7:36-39, 44-50

One of the Pharisees asked Jesus to eat with him, and he [Jesus] went into the Pharisee's house and took his place at the table. And a woman in the city, who was a sinner, having learned that he was eating in the Pharisee's house, brought an alabaster jar of ointment. She stood behind him at his feet, weeping, and began to bathe his feet with her tears and to dry them with her hair. Then she continued kissing his feet and anointing them with the ointment. Now when the Pharisee who had invited him saw it, he said to himself, "If this man were a prophet, he would have known who and what kind of woman this is who is touching him—that she is a sinner." . . .

Then turning toward the woman, [Jesus] said to Simon, "Do you see this woman? I entered your house; you gave me no water for my feet, but she has bathed my feet with her tears and dried them with her hair. You gave me no kiss, but from the time I came in she has not stopped kissing my feet. You did not anoint my head with oil, but she has anointed my feet with ointment. Therefore, I tell you, her sins, which were many, have been forgiven; hence she has shown great love. But the one to whom little is forgiven, loves little." Then he said to her, "Your sins are forgiven." But those who were at the table with him began to say among themselves, "Who is this who even forgives sins?" And he said to the woman, "Your faith has saved you; go in peace."

The Gospel of the Lord.

REFLECTION
When have you felt the power of forgiveness in your life?

INTERCESSIONS
Just and merciful God, you are our refuge in our shame. Help us turn our faces to you so that we may know your forgiveness. And so we pray: *Gracious God, renew our hearts to love your world.*

- Teach us gratitude for the times when others have shown us forbearance and let us do the same. *We pray to the Lord.*
- Like the woman who washed and anointed Jesus' feet, show us how we have failed to cherish God's gift of creation. *We pray to the Lord.*
- Transform our hearts toward an ecology of gift. *We pray to the Lord.*

THE LORD'S PRAYER
With these petitions in our hearts and on our lips, we pray as our brother Jesus taught us: Our Father . . .

SIGN OF PEACE
As a sign of peace, Living God, we offer you our open arms and hopeful faces to welcome your saving grace. May your peace rest on us.

CLOSING BLESSING
May God's lavish love take root anew in our hearts. We ask this in Christ's name. AMEN

WEEK THREE

MONDAY MORNING

☦

Giver of Life, animate our hearts;
inspire us to renew your creation.

PSALM 19:7-10
℟ In this season of your mercy, O Lord, call us back to life.

The law of the Lord is perfect,
    reviving the soul;
the decrees of the Lord are sure,
    making wise the simple;
the precepts of the Lord are right,
    rejoicing the heart;
the commandment of the Lord is clear,
    enlightening the eyes;
the fear of the Lord is pure,
    enduring forever;
the ordinances of the Lord are true
    and righteous altogether.
More to be desired are they than gold,
    even much fine gold;

sweeter also than honey,
  and drippings of the honeycomb.

Glory . . .

SCRIPTURE   Leviticus 19:9-10, 13-14

When you reap the harvest of your land, you shall not reap to the very edges of your field, or gather the gleanings of your harvest. You shall not strip your vineyard bare, or gather the fallen grapes of your vineyard; you shall leave them for the poor and the alien: I am the Lord your God. . . .

You shall not defraud your neighbor; you shall not steal; and you shall not keep for yourself the wages of a laborer until morning. You shall not revile the deaf or put a stumbling block before the blind; you shall fear your God: I am the Lord.

The word of the Lord.

INTERCESSIONS

God of all creation, we flourish as a human community only when we give away to each other the love and life that we receive from you. And so we pray: *Source of Life, may your life flow through us and bear fruit.*

- Absolve us for the times we have hoarded the abundance of your world, and instruct us in the practices of giving. *We pray to the Lord.*

- Move us to model for and with one another a community grounded on an ecology of gift, rather than scarcity. *We pray to the Lord.*
- May we hear your call to distribute your gifts unstintingly and respond with joy. *We pray to the Lord.*

THE LORD'S PRAYER
With these petitions in our hearts and on our lips, we pray as our brother Jesus taught us: Our Father . . .

SIGN OF PEACE
As a sign of peace, Living God, we offer you our open arms and hopeful faces to welcome your saving grace. May your peace rest on us.

CLOSING BLESSING
May God's justice guide our minds and hearts to care for vulnerable people and creatures in our midst. May God's justice flow through us into all creation. We ask this in Christ's name. AMEN

WEEK THREE

MONDAY EVENING

Giver of Life, animate our hearts;
inspire us to renew your creation.

PSALM 93:1-2, 5
℟ In this season of your mercy, O Lord, call us back to life.

The Lord is king, he is robed in majesty;
  the Lord is robed, he is girded with strength.
He has established the world; it shall never be moved;
  your throne is established from of old;
  you are from everlasting. . . .

Your decrees are very sure;
  holiness befits your house,
  O Lord, forevermore.

Glory . . .

SCRIPTURE   Matthew 22:34-40
When the Pharisees heard that he had silenced the Sadducees, they gathered together, and one of them, a lawyer, asked him a question to test him. "Teacher, which commandment in the law is the greatest?" He said to him,

"'You shall love the Lord your God with all your heart, and with all your soul, and with all your mind.' This is the greatest and first commandment. And a second is like it: 'You shall love your neighbor as yourself.' On these two commandments hang all the law and the prophets."

The Gospel of the Lord.

REFLECTION
What would loving the environment as yourself look like?

INTERCESSIONS
God of all creation, you revealed love as the heart of your law. Help us grow beyond ourselves in wholehearted care for your world. And so we pray: *Source of Life, may your life flow through us and bear fruit.*

- Help us to recognize and resist the structures of exploitation that burden the poorest among us. *We pray to the Lord.*
- Open our hearts to welcome animals, insects, and plants as companions in life. *We pray to the Lord.*
- Dampen our pride through the awareness that we, like all human beings, are vulnerable and aching for love. *We pray to the Lord.*

THE LORD'S PRAYER
With these petitions in our hearts, we pray as our brother Jesus taught us: Our Father . . .

SIGN OF PEACE
As a sign of peace, Living God, we offer you our open arms and hopeful faces to welcome your saving grace. May your peace rest on us.

CLOSING BLESSING
May God, the source of eternal love, nurture in our hearts a deep compassion for all living beings. We ask this in Christ's name. AMEN

WEEK THREE

TUESDAY MORNING

✝

Giver of Life, animate our hearts;
inspire us to renew your creation.

PSALM 33:13-15, 18-22
℟ In this season of your mercy, O Lord, call us back to life.

The Lord looks down from heaven;
   he sees all humankind.
From where he sits enthroned he watches
   all the inhabitants of the earth—
he who fashions the hearts of them all,
   and observes all their deeds. . . .

Truly the eye of the Lord is on those who fear him,
   on those who hope in his steadfast love,
to deliver their soul from death,
   and to keep them alive in famine.

Our soul waits for the Lord;
   he is our help and shield.
Our heart is glad in him,
   because we trust in his holy name.

Healing Creation *Tuesday Morning*

Let your steadfast love, O Lord, be upon us,
   even as we hope in you.

Glory . . .

SCRIPTURE   1 Kings 17:8-16
Then the word of the Lord came to [Elijah], saying, "Go now to Zarephath, which belongs to Sidon, and live there; for I have commanded a widow there to feed you." So he set out and went to Zarephath. When he came to the gate of the town, a widow was there gathering sticks; he called to her and said, "Bring me a little water in a vessel, so that I may drink." As she was going to bring it, he called to her and said, "Bring me a morsel of bread in your hand." But she said, "As the Lord your God lives, I have nothing baked, only a handful of meal in a jar, and a little oil in a jug; I am now gathering a couple of sticks, so that I may go home and prepare it for myself and my son, that we may eat it, and die." Elijah said to her, "Do not be afraid; go and do as you have said; but first make me a little cake of it and bring it to me, and afterwards make something for yourself and your son. For thus says the Lord the God of Israel: The jar of meal will not be emptied and the jug of oil will not fail until the day that the Lord sends rain on the earth." She went and did as Elijah said, so that she as well as he and her household ate for many days. The jar of meal was not emptied, neither did the jug of oil fail, according to the word of the Lord that he spoke by Elijah.

The word of the Lord.

INTERCESSIONS

Generous God, because the widow faithfully shared all she had with Elijah, you sustained her with oil and meal. Give us the generosity to share what we have that all may thrive. And so we pray: *Wellspring of Hope, bestow on us your living wisdom.*

- Grant us the courage to trust that God's life will sustain us and our world as we struggle to forge a new ecology of generosity. *We pray to the Lord.*

- Provide patience for the anxious, balm for those who suffer, and food for all who hunger as we await the renewal of creation. *We pray to the Lord.*

- Comfort your people who live generously, so that they never despair of receiving salvation for the earth and all its creatures. *We pray to the Lord.*

THE LORD'S PRAYER

With these petitions in our hearts, we pray as our brother Jesus taught us: Our Father . . .

SIGN OF PEACE

As a sign of peace, Living God, we offer you our open arms and hopeful faces to welcome your saving grace. May your peace rest on us.

CLOSING BLESSING
May the Holy Spirit strengthen our hope and amplify our faith so that today we embrace the ecology of God, which depends on gift and gratitude. We ask this in Christ's name. AMEN

WEEK THREE

TUESDAY EVENING

Giver of Life, animate our hearts;
inspire us to renew your creation.

PSALM 33:1-5
℟ In this season of your mercy, O Lord, call us back to life.

Rejoice in the Lord, O you righteous.
   Praise befits the upright.
Praise the Lord with the lyre;
   make melody to him with the harp of ten strings.
Sing to him a new song;
   play skillfully on the strings, with loud shouts.

For the word of the Lord is upright,
   and all his work is done in faithfulness.
He loves righteousness and justice;
   the earth is full of the steadfast love of the Lord.

Glory . . .

SCRIPTURE   Matthew 14:13-21
Now when Jesus heard this, he withdrew from there in a boat to a deserted place by himself. But when the crowds heard it, they followed him on foot from the

towns. When he went ashore, he saw a great crowd; and he had compassion for them and cured their sick. When it was evening, the disciples came to him and said, "This is a deserted place, and the hour is now late; send the crowds away so that they may go into the villages and buy food for themselves." Jesus said to them, "They need not go away; you give them something to eat." They replied, "We have nothing here but five loaves and two fish." And he said, "Bring them here to me." Then he ordered the crowds to sit down on the grass. Taking the five loaves and the two fish, he looked up to heaven, and blessed and broke the loaves, and gave them to the disciples, and the disciples gave them to the crowds. And all ate and were filled; and they took up what was left over of the broken pieces, twelve baskets full. And those who ate were about five thousand men, besides women and children.

The Gospel of the Lord.

REFLECTION
When you have shared your resources and talents with others, what has been their response?

INTERCESSIONS
Generous God, your Son instructs us: "They need not go away; you give them something to eat." The everyday miracle in the gospels is that generosity births generosity. And so we pray: *Wellspring of Hope, bestow on us your living wisdom.*

- Give us the courage to make the health of our brothers and sisters a nonnegotiable priority for all community decisions. *We pray to the Lord.*
- Open our eyes to the physical, emotional, and spiritual hunger of our fellow beings. *We pray to the Lord.*
- Reveal to us the connection between our actions and the world's ruptures, so that we may be moved to restore the earth's balance. *We pray to the Lord.*

THE LORD'S PRAYER
With these petitions in our hearts, we pray as our brother Jesus taught us: Our Father . . .

SIGN OF PEACE
As a sign of peace, Living God, we offer you our open arms and hopeful faces to welcome your saving grace. May your peace rest on us.

CLOSING BLESSING
May the Spirit of hope convert our hearts to heal the planet until that day when the earth flourishes and all people thrive. We ask this in Christ's name. AMEN

WEEK THREE

WEDNESDAY MORNING

Giver of Life, animate our hearts;
inspire us to renew your creation.

PSALM 92:1-4
℟ In this season of your mercy, O Lord, call us back to life.

It is good to give thanks to the Lord,
  to sing praises to your name, O Most High;
to declare your steadfast love in the morning,
  and your faithfulness by night,
to the music of the lute and the harp,
  to the melody of the lyre.
For you, O Lord, have made me glad by your work;
  at the works of your hands I sing for joy.

Glory . . .

SCRIPTURE Isaiah 35:4-7

Say to those who are of a fearful heart,
 "Be strong, do not fear!
Here is your God.
 He will come with vengeance,
with terrible recompense.
 He will come and save you."

Then the eyes of the blind shall be opened,
 and the ears of the deaf unstopped;
then the lame shall leap like a deer,
 and the tongue of the speechless sing for joy.
For waters shall break forth in the wilderness,
 and streams in the desert;
the burning sand shall become a pool,
 and the thirsty ground springs of water;
the haunt of jackals shall become a swamp,
 the grass shall become reeds and rushes.

The word of the Lord.

INTERCESSIONS

Compassionate God, your salvation for us means healing and joy. For our world, redemption brings refreshment and abundance. And so we pray: *Renewing Spirit, guide us into your new creation.*

- Strengthen our resolve to address the drought and heat that are plaguing our earth and desiccating our human communities. *We pray to the Lord.*

- Teach us to weigh well the claims of all life and all people to flourish and reveal God's breathtaking beauty and abundant generosity. *We pray to the Lord.*
- Refresh our weary spirits and water our parched land so that we may dance with joy for the cosmic redemption promised in Christ. *We pray to the Lord.*

THE LORD'S PRAYER
With these petitions in our hearts, we pray as our brother Jesus taught us: Our Father . . .

SIGN OF PEACE
As a sign of peace, Living God, we offer you our open arms and hopeful faces to welcome your saving grace. May your peace rest on us.

CLOSING PRAYER
May God's delight in creation be ours today. May God's joy in life be ours today. And may God's steadfast love prosper the work of our hands this day. We ask this in Christ's name. AMEN

WEEK THREE

WEDNESDAY EVENING

✝

Giver of Life, animate our hearts;
inspire us to renew your creation.

PSALM 121:1-8
℟ In this season of your mercy, O Lord, call us back to life.

I lift up my eyes to the hills—
    from where will my help come?
My help comes from the Lord,
    who made heaven and earth.

He will not let your foot be moved;
    he who keeps you will not slumber.
He who keeps Israel
    will neither slumber nor sleep.

The Lord is your keeper;
    the Lord is your shade at your right hand.
The sun shall not strike you by day,
    nor the moon by night.

The Lord will keep you from all evil;
    he will keep your life.

Healing Creation   *Wednesday Evening*

The Lord will keep
  your going out and your coming in
  from this time on and forevermore.

Glory . . .

SCRIPTURE   Mark 8:22-25

They came to Bethsaida. Some people brought a blind man to [Jesus] and begged him to touch him. He took the blind man by the hand and led him out of the village; and when he had put saliva on his eyes and laid his hands on him, he asked him, "Can you see anything?" And the man looked up and said, "I can see people, but they look like trees, walking." Then Jesus laid his hands on his eyes again; and he looked intently and his sight was restored, and he saw everything clearly.

The Gospel of the Lord.

REFLECTION

As you gaze upon the world around you with new sight, what impresses you? What troubles you?

INTERCESSIONS

Compassionate God, the psalmist reminds us that you watch over our every movement and actively protect us from evil. Still we have squandered your gift and need redemption from your hand. And so we pray: *Renewing Spirit, guide us into your new creation.*

- Make us clear-sighted about the impact of our choices upon the land and the waters. *We pray to the Lord.*
- Unite our hearts for the restoration of a living justice to govern our communities. *We pray to the Lord.*
- Grant us peace from our distorted desires that compel us to conquer the earth rather than nurture its bounty. *We pray to the Lord.*

THE LORD'S PRAYER
With these petitions in our hearts, we pray as our brother Jesus taught us: Our Father . . .

SIGN OF PEACE
As a sign of peace, Living God, we offer you our open arms and hopeful faces to welcome your saving grace. May your peace rest on us.

CLOSING PRAYER
May we humbly trust our well-being to God's holy protection so that we are liberated to strive for justice throughout all the earth. We ask this in Christ's name. AMEN

WEEK THREE

THURSDAY MORNING

✝

Giver of Life, animate our hearts;
inspire us to renew your creation.

PSALM 104:24, 27, 29-34
℟ In this season of your mercy, O Lord, call us back to life.

O Lord, how manifold are your works!
   In wisdom you have made them all;
   the earth is full of your creatures. . . .

These all look to you
   to give them their food in due season . . .
When you hide your face, they are dismayed;
   when you take away their breath, they die
   and return to their dust.
When you send forth your spirit, they are created;
   and you renew the face of the ground.

May the glory of the Lord endure forever;
   may the Lord rejoice in his works—
who looks on the earth and it trembles,
   who touches the mountains and they smoke.

I will sing to the Lord as long as I live;
  I will sing praise to my God while I have being.
May my meditation be pleasing to him,
  for I rejoice in the Lord.

Glory . . .

SCRIPTURE   Ezekiel 37:3-6, 10

[The Lord] said to me, "Mortal, can these bones live?" I answered, "O Lord God, you know." Then he said to me, "Prophesy to these bones, and say to them: O dry bones, hear the word of the Lord. Thus says the Lord God to these bones: I will cause breath to enter you, and you shall live. I will lay sinews on you, and will cause flesh to come upon you, and cover you with skin, and put breath in you, and you shall live; and you shall know that I am the Lord." . . . I prophesied as he commanded me, and the breath came into them, and they lived, and stood on their feet, a vast multitude.

The word of the Lord.

INTERCESSIONS

God, source of all life, you call creation out of darkness into existence, and you breathe your human creatures into life. Nothing is impossible for you, not even forgiving our transgressions. And so we pray: *Holy Wisdom, grace us with abundant hope.*

- Come swiftly to safeguard those communities and lands decimated by ecological crises caused by the heedlessness of people with means. *We pray to the Lord.*
- Multiply our meager efforts to restore the planet from the wasteland we have fashioned. *We pray to the Lord.*
- Do not hide your face from us, but renew our determination to make amends for the ecologies and communities we have plundered. *We pray to the Lord.*

THE LORD'S PRAYER
With these petitions in our hearts, we pray as our brother Jesus taught us: Our Father . . .

SIGN OF PEACE
As a sign of peace, Living God, we offer you our open arms and hopeful faces to welcome your saving grace. May your peace rest on us.

CLOSING PRAYER
May the Holy One of Israel revive the dry bones of our hearts, our communities, and our lands. May living water redeem us and bring us back into one body, one communion of care. We ask this in Christ's name. AMEN

WEEK THREE

THURSDAY EVENING

✝

Giver of Life, animate our hearts;
inspire us to renew your creation.

PSALM 30:2-5, 10-12
℟ In this season of your mercy, O Lord, call us back to life.

O Lord my God, I cried to you for help,
    and you have healed me.
O Lord, you brought up my soul from Sheol,
    restored me to life from among those gone down to
        the Pit.

Sing praises to the Lord, O you his faithful ones,
    and give thanks to his holy name.
For his anger is but for a moment;
    his favor is for a lifetime.
Weeping may linger for the night,
    but joy comes with the morning. . . .

"Hear, O Lord, and be gracious to me!
    O Lord, be my helper!"

You have turned my mourning into dancing;
    you have taken off my sackcloth
    and clothed me with joy,

so that my soul may praise you and not be silent.
O Lord my God, I will give thanks to you forever.

Glory . . .

SCRIPTURE   Luke 8:40-42, 49-55
Now when Jesus returned, the crowd welcomed him, for they were all waiting for him. Just then there came a man named Jairus, a leader of the synagogue. He fell at Jesus' feet and begged him to come to his house, for he had an only daughter, about twelve years old, who was dying. . . .

While he was still speaking, someone came from the leader's house to say, "Your daughter is dead; do not trouble the teacher any longer." When Jesus heard this, he replied, "Do not fear. Only believe, and she will be saved." When he came to the house, he did not allow anyone to enter with him, except Peter, John, and James, and the child's father and mother. They were all weeping and wailing for her; but he said, "Do not weep; for she is not dead but sleeping." And they laughed at him, knowing that she was dead. But he took her by the hand and called out, "Child, get up!" Her spirit returned, and she got up at once. Then he directed them to give her something to eat.

The Gospel of the Lord.

REFLECTION
When have you felt truly liberated from a weight on your shoulders?

INTERCESSIONS

God of hope, over and over again the scriptures testify to the liberation you unceasingly offer your people. Again our earth cries for your saving help. And so we pray: *Holy Wisdom, grace us with abundant hope.*

- Soften our hearts so that we might return to your ecology of gift and grace. *We pray to the Lord.*
- Bless those who practice ecological stewardship and amplify the fruits of their labors. *We pray to the Lord.*
- Teach us solidarity and kinship with people who live near us, so that we may be neighbors in your ecology of gift. *We pray to the Lord.*

THE LORD'S PRAYER

With these petitions in our hearts, we pray as our brother Jesus taught us: Our Father . . .

SIGN OF PEACE

As a sign of peace, Living God, we offer you our open arms and hopeful faces to welcome your saving grace. May your peace rest on us.

CLOSING PRAYER

May our God of everlasting compassion remain with us in our hour of need. May hope return to strengthen our hearts and guide our actions to heal the suffering in the world. We ask this in Christ's name. AMEN

WEEK THREE

FRIDAY MORNING

✝

Giver of Life, animate our hearts;
inspire us to renew your creation.

PSALM 16:7-11
℟ In this season of your mercy, O Lord, call us back to life.

I bless the Lord who gives me counsel;
   in the night also my heart instructs me.
I keep the Lord always before me;
   because he is at my right hand, I shall not be moved.

Therefore my heart is glad, and my soul rejoices;
   my body also rests secure.
For you do not give me up to Sheol,
   or let your faithful one see the Pit.

You show me the path of life.
   In your presence there is fullness of joy;
   in your right hand are pleasures forevermore.

Glory . . .

SCRIPTURE   Isaiah 42:1-5

Here is my servant, whom I uphold,
   my chosen, in whom my soul delights;
I have put my spirit upon him;
   he will bring forth justice to the nations.
He will not cry or lift up his voice,
   or make it heard in the street;
a bruised reed he will not break,
   and a dimly burning wick he will not quench;
   he will faithfully bring forth justice.
He will not grow faint or be crushed
   until he has established justice in the earth;
   and the coastlands wait for his teaching.

Thus says God, the Lord,
   who created the heavens and stretched them out,
   who spread out the earth and what comes from it,
who gives breath to the people upon it
   and spirit to those who walk in it[.]

The word of the Lord.

INTERCESSIONS

God of all kindness, you never abandon your creatures, even when we've lost our way. May we be counted among your faithful servants so that our works might bring your ecology of grace into flourishing. And so we pray: *Merciful God, renew your life in us.*

Healing Creation   *Friday Morning*

- Teach us to be your breath of hope and spirit of life for the earth and all people who walk upon it. *We pray to the Lord.*
- Deliver suffering communities across the globe from the storms of climate devastation through the urgent conversion of all nations to an ecology of gift. *We pray to the Lord.*
- Do not delay your healing help for this planet we call our common home. *We pray to the Lord.*

THE LORD'S PRAYER
With these petitions in our hearts, we pray as our brother Jesus taught us: Our Father . . .

SIGN OF PEACE
As a sign of peace, Living God, we offer you our open arms and hopeful faces to welcome your saving grace. May your peace rest on us.

CLOSING PRAYER
May the endless mercy of our God inspire us to live justly today in harmony with all beings who live and move on this earth. May our steadfast God shelter us and save us all. We ask this in Christ's name. AMEN

WEEK THREE

FRIDAY EVENING

✝

Giver of Life, animate our hearts;
inspire us to renew your creation.

PSALM 23:1-6
℟ In this season of your mercy, O Lord, call us back to life.

The LORD is my shepherd, I shall not want.
    He makes me lie down in green pastures;
he leads me beside still waters;
    he restores my soul.
He leads me in right paths
    for his name's sake.

Even though I walk through the darkest valley,
    I fear no evil;
for you are with me;
    your rod and your staff—
    they comfort me.

You prepare a table before me
    in the presence of my enemies;
you anoint my head with oil;
    my cup overflows.

Surely goodness and mercy shall follow me
   all the days of my life,
and I shall dwell in the house of the LORD
   my whole life long.

Glory . . .

SCRIPTURE John 13:3-9, 12-15

Jesus, knowing that the Father had given all things into his hands, and that he had come from God and was going to God, got up from the table, took off his outer robe, and tied a towel around himself. Then he poured water into a basin and began to wash the disciples' feet and to wipe them with the towel that was tied around him. He came to Simon Peter, who said to him, "Lord, are you going to wash my feet?" Jesus answered, "You do not know now what I am doing, but later you will understand." Peter said to him, "You will never wash my feet." Jesus answered, "Unless I wash you, you have no share with me." Simon Peter said to him, "Lord, not my feet only but also my hands and my head!" . . .

After he had washed their feet, had put on his robe, and had returned to the table, he said to them, "Do you know what I have done to you? You call me Teacher and Lord—and you are right, for that is what I am. So if I, your Lord and Teacher, have washed your feet, you also ought to wash one another's feet. For I have set you an example, that you also should do as I have done to you."

The Gospel of the Lord.

REFLECTION
Think of a time when you have been a servant or served another person with tender compassion for their needs and well-being.

INTERCESSIONS
God of all kindness, your Son washed his disciples' feet to show them what tender care looks and feels like. He emptied himself to love us fully so that we may do the same. And so we pray: *Merciful God, renew your life in us.*

- Remind us of our human vulnerability, which Jesus shared and loved. *We pray to the Lord.*
- Through the work of our hands, grant peace to our turbulent world where we vie for air, water, food, and space. *We pray to the Lord.*
- Rouse your compassion in us and let us never tire of caring for our common home and all life that depends upon its bounty. *We pray to the Lord.*

THE LORD'S PRAYER
With these petitions in our hearts, we pray as our brother Jesus taught us: Our Father . . .

SIGN OF PEACE
As a sign of peace, Living God, we offer you our open arms and hopeful faces to welcome your saving grace. May your peace rest on us.

CLOSING PRAYER

Secure in the mercy of our God, may we today share in Christ's radical love that issues in service for each other's most human needs. May we dwell in the ecology of God with every creature together all the days of our lives. We ask this in Christ's name. AMEN

WEEK THREE

SATURDAY MORNING

✝

Giver of Life, animate our hearts;
inspire us to renew your creation.

PSALM 31:14-16, 19-21b
℟ In the season of your mercy, O Lord, redeem our wayward lives.

But I trust in you, O Lord;
 I say, "You are my God."
My times are in your hand;
 deliver me from the hand of my enemies and persecutors.
Let your face shine upon your servant;
 save me in your steadfast love. . . .

O how abundant is your goodness
 that you have laid up for those who fear you,
and accomplished for those who take refuge in you,
 in the sight of everyone!
In the shelter of your presence you hide them
 from human plots;
you hold them safe under your shelter
 from contentious tongues.

Blessed be the Lord,
   for he has wondrously shown his steadfast love to me.

Glory . . .

SCRIPTURE   Jeremiah 31:3, 33-34
[T]he Lord appeared to him from far away.
I have loved you with an everlasting love;
   therefore I have continued my faithfulness to
      you. . . .

But this is the covenant that I will make with the house of Israel after those days, says the Lord: I will put my law within them, and I will write it on their hearts; and I will be their God, and they shall be my people. No longer shall they teach one another, or say to each other, "Know the Lord," for they shall all know me, from the least of them to the greatest, says the Lord; for I will forgive their iniquity, and remember their sin no more.

The word of the Lord.

INTERCESSIONS
God of all living things, the psalmist praises your abundant mercy and the salvation you offer us. That salvation includes welcoming us as your people, when you place your law as a seal upon our hearts. And so we pray: *God of Life, we long to dwell in your new creation.*

- Convert our actions to conform to your law of love and your ecology of gift. *We pray to the Lord.*
- Rouse our fight for the well-being of the most vulnerable among us by seeking just economies and healthy ecosystems. *We pray to the Lord.*
- Show us yourself in the beauty of creation and in the fragility of our human condition so that we take your law of love to heart. *We pray to the Lord.*

THE LORD'S PRAYER
With these petitions in our hearts, we pray as our brother Jesus taught us: Our Father . . .

SIGN OF PEACE
As a sign of peace, Living God, we offer you our open arms and hopeful faces to welcome your saving grace. May your peace rest on us.

CLOSING PRAYER
May God, who authors and grounds the eternal law of love, guide us together into a holy dwelling place where justice and peace abound. We ask this in Christ's name. AMEN

WEEK THREE

SATURDAY EVENING

Giver of Life, animate our hearts;
inspire us to renew your creation.

PSALM 100:1-5
℟ In the season of your mercy, O Lord, redeem our wayward lives.

Make a joyful noise to the Lord, all the earth.
 Worship the Lord with gladness;
 come into his presence with singing.

Know that the Lord is God.
 It is he that made us, and we are his;
 we are his people, and the sheep of his pasture.

Enter his gates with thanksgiving,
 and his courts with praise.
 Give thanks to him, bless his name.

For the Lord is good;
 his steadfast love endures forever,
 and his faithfulness to all generations.

Glory . . .

SCRIPTURE   Luke 22:14-20

When the hour came, [Jesus] took his place at the table, and the apostles with him. He said to them, "I have eagerly desired to eat this Passover with you before I suffer; for I tell you, I will not eat it until it is fulfilled in the kingdom of God." Then he took a cup, and after giving thanks he said, "Take this and divide it among yourselves; for I tell you that from now on I will not drink of the fruit of the vine until the kingdom of God comes." Then he took a loaf of bread, and when he had given thanks, he broke it and gave it to them, saying, "This is my body, which is given for you. Do this in remembrance of me." And he did the same with the cup after supper, saying, "This cup that is poured out for you is the new covenant in my blood."

The Gospel of the Lord.

REFLECTION

How do you live in communion with Jesus and others, in remembrance of him?

INTERCESSIONS

God of all living things, we are yours as you invite us into a new covenant of life poured out for one another. When we receive your holy communion, we receive your peace that nothing can disturb. But we need to say "yes" to your life. And so we pray: *God of Life, we long to dwell in your new creation.*

- Make our hands your hands to alleviate the impacts of climate change and usher in a more integral ecology. *We pray to the Lord.*
- Welcome into your open arms all those who will breathe their last today. *We pray to the Lord.*
- Call us once again into communion with you and give us the grace we need to accept the new covenant in Christ. *We pray to the Lord.*

THE LORD'S PRAYER
With these petitions in our hearts, we pray as our brother Jesus taught us: Our Father . . .

SIGN OF PEACE
As a sign of peace, Living God, we offer you our open arms and hopeful faces to welcome your saving grace. May your peace rest on us.

CLOSING PRAYER
May we find peace for our restless hearts in loving one another as Christ loves us. May we trust in your gracious gift of abundant life and make your ecology of grace a reality in our day. We ask this in Christ's name. AMEN

Final Thoughts on Healing Creation: Accepting Christ's Salvation

In Christian life, we are not saved merely *from* estrangement with God, others, and creation, but we are saved *for* the work of laboring in creation. In this week, the salvation of God has been shown to us as the restoring of right relationships, a renewal of bonds that encompasses the whole of the created order. We are saved *for* our role to labor in the ecology of God, work that calls us into greater and greater intimacy with God and into kinship with each other. As pilgrims in the ecology of God, we come to know ourselves and our fellow pilgrims more truly by walking the way of Christ's healing, regenerative love.

Although in our redemption, we bear the scars of our alienation from self, from others, from nature, and from God, we learn to trust that the risen Christ is with us. Christ invites and guides us into life-giving relationship with the earth and all it holds. We receive grace to join in the cosmic cultivation of life.

As we move to Week Four, we behold the restored contours of God's ecology. We seek an epiphany, a vision of the Holy One, which will serve as a guide for our labors. Still, epiphany, like salvation, is not a moment but a process. The process of epiphany is coming to see the face of Christ in a stranger, the dance of the Spirit in a flock of birds in flight, and the maternity of God in the fierce and tender love of animals for their offspring. Week

Four ushers us into the epiphany of creation's renewal, which is our birthright and our vocation. In this final week, we are invited to devote ourselves to the service and cultivation of God's ecology.

WEEK FOUR

ESTABLISHING THE RENEWED CREATION

Cultivating Life

How do we live in the already-but-not-yet ecology of God? This week's readings show us the contours of the world of God's gift and grace. It is an ecology marked by cooperation, growth, and the promise of resurrection. We step into our role as servant-cultivators to foster the flourishing of all that is when we labor to heal and renew human relationships with one another, with the earth, and with God. As we labor, we see God's ecology become manifest, plain for everyone who has eyes to see. Our response to the divine gift of creation is gratitude as well as a yearning to behold the renewal of the world.

The morning readings highlight epiphanies of God. God meets Moses at the burning bush. In the ecology of God, this fire is a gift that does not have a price: the bush is not consumed. Ezekiel announces a new covenant in which human beings and wild creatures live in peace.

Harmony replaces competition. In Isaiah, God proclaims, "I am about to do a new thing," Further, humankind hears "arise, shine," for we also shall be radiant, lit up in the fiery light of God's glory. These readings invite us to watch for the fulfillment of God's promise, and inscribe its coming in letters so big that a far-off runner could make them out. We shout to all the world of the new thing God is doing, so that others may cultivate life and join in the feast too.

Our evening readings explore Jesus' resurrected life and how we might embody it in our lives now. To be resurrected is not merely to be resuscitated; it is rather to live in the ecology of God on this earth. The risen Jesus models resurrected life among us. The pain and alienation of death are overcome when he meets Mary and calls her by name, out of grief into gladness. The risen Jesus accompanies the disciples on the road to Emmaus. He makes himself known to them in the simple way travelers end a day as they break bread. The abundance of life in the resurrection leads to a miraculous catch of almost more fish than the nets could hold, and a joyous feast ensues.

Every reading in this chapter discloses a facet of the renewed creation. We are called to collaborate in the new world God is creating. We shall be branches drawing life from the true vine and bearing fruit in abundance. We see, already but not yet, the blessing that God bestows on the poor and marginalized. In the resurrected life of God's ecology, we shall join that blessed community. We all shall have a place in the ecology of God.

WEEK FOUR

SUNDAY MORNING

✝

Giver of Life, animate our hearts;
inspire us to renew your creation.

PSALM 37:3-9
℟ May we dwell in the house of the Lord all our lives.

Trust in the Lord, and do good;
   so you will live in the land, and enjoy security.
Take delight in the Lord,
   and he will give you the desires of your heart.

Commit your way to the Lord;
   trust in him, and he will act.
He will make your vindication shine like the light,
   and the justice of your cause like the noonday.

Be still before the Lord, and wait patiently for him;
   do not fret over those who prosper in their way,
   over those who carry out evil devices.

Refrain from anger, and forsake wrath.
   Do not fret—it leads only to evil.

For the wicked shall be cut off,
> but those who wait for the Lord shall inherit the land.

Glory . . .

SCRIPTURE   Isaiah 43:18-21

Do not remember the former things,
> or consider the things of old.

I am about to do a new thing;
> now it springs forth, do you not perceive it?

I will make a way in the wilderness
> and rivers in the desert.

The wild animals will honor me,
> the jackals and the ostriches;

for I give water in the wilderness,
> rivers in the desert,

to give drink to my chosen people,
> the people whom I formed for myself

so that they might declare my praise.

The word of the Lord.

INTERCESSIONS

Generous God, every moment of every day your love springs forth as life and plenty to sustain us. But so often our greed drives us to hoard our resources rather than imitate your generosity and love. And so we pray: *Gracious God, renew our hearts to love your world.*

- Open our eyes to the abundance of creation in the humblest flowers as well as the grandest vistas. *We pray to the Lord.*
- When all ways ahead of us seem to be rubble and ruin, let us choose a stance of hope that will become your new way. *We pray to the Lord.*
- May our lives become beacons of resilience and light for people around us. *We pray to the Lord.*

THE LORD'S PRAYER
With these petitions in our hearts, we pray as our brother Jesus taught us: Our Father . . .

SIGN OF PEACE
As a sign of peace, Living God, we offer to you our upraised hands in joyous recognition that every moment you are creating life and revealing your love. May your peace rest on us.

CLOSING PRAYER
Living God, enkindle in us the trust and courage to walk in your ways, as you are about to do a new thing. We ask this in Christ's name. AMEN

WEEK FOUR

SUNDAY EVENING

✝

Giver of Life, animate our hearts;
inspire us to renew your creation.

PSALM 98:1-9
℟ May we dwell in the house of the Lord all our lives.

O sing to the Lord a new song,
    for he has done marvelous things.
His right hand and his holy arm
    have gotten him victory.
The Lord has made known his victory;
    he has revealed his vindication in the sight of the nations.
He has remembered his steadfast love and faithfulness
    to the house of Israel.
All the ends of the earth have seen
    the victory of our God.

Make a joyful noise to the Lord, all the earth;
    break forth into joyous song and sing praises.
Sing praises to the Lord with the lyre,
    with the lyre and the sound of melody.
With trumpets and the sound of the horn
    make a joyful noise before the King, the Lord.

Let the sea roar, and all that fills it;
   the world and those who live in it.
Let the floods clap their hands;
   let the hills sing together for joy
at the presence of the Lord, for he is coming
   to judge the earth.
He will judge the world with righteousness,
   and the peoples with equity.

Glory . . .

SCRIPTURE   Matthew 28:1-6
After the sabbath, as the first day of the week was dawning, Mary Magdalene and the other Mary went to see the tomb. And suddenly there was a great earthquake; for an angel of the Lord, descending from heaven, came and rolled back the stone and sat on it. His appearance was like lightning, and his clothing white as snow. For fear of him the guards shook and became like dead men. But the angel said to the women, "Do not be afraid; I know that you are looking for Jesus who was crucified. He is not here; for he has been raised, as he said."

The Gospel of the Lord.

REFLECTION
Where do you seek the living Christ?

INTERCESSIONS
Loving God, your angel said to Mary, "Do not be afraid." In your new creation, every tear will be wiped away, and no terrors will blind us to the light of your love. We yearn for the dawn of that day. And so we pray: *Gracious God, renew our hearts to love your world.*

- May we trust in your steadfast love all our days. *We pray to the Lord.*
- Create in us a vision of your new creation, so we may diligently seek its coming. *We pray to the Lord.*
- Enkindle in us the fire we need to work for the preservation of your earth. *We pray to the Lord.*

THE LORD'S PRAYER
With these petitions in our hearts, we pray as our brother Jesus taught us: Our Father . . .

SIGN OF PEACE
As a sign of peace, Living God, we offer to you our upraised hands in joyous recognition that every moment you are creating life and revealing your love. May your peace rest on us.

CLOSING PRAYER
God of all faithfulness, bless us as we end this day. May the dawn find us rested and eager to see your face in our neighbors and all your creation. We ask this in Christ's name. AMEN

WEEK FOUR

MONDAY MORNING

✝

Giver of Life, animate our hearts;
inspire us to renew your creation.

PSALM 29:3-8
℟ May we dwell in the house of the Lord all our lives.

The voice of the Lord is over the waters;
   the God of glory thunders,
   the Lord, over mighty waters.
The voice of the Lord is powerful;
   the voice of the Lord is full of majesty.

The voice of the Lord breaks the cedars;
   the Lord breaks the cedars of Lebanon.
He makes Lebanon skip like a calf,
   and Sirion like a young wild ox.

The voice of the Lord flashes forth flames of fire.
The voice of the Lord shakes the wilderness;
   the Lord shakes the wilderness of Kadesh.

Glory . . .

SCRIPTURE   Exodus 3:1-5

Moses was keeping the flock of his father-in-law Jethro, the priest of Midian; he led his flock beyond the wilderness, and came to Horeb, the mountain of God. There the angel of the Lord appeared to him in a flame of fire out of a bush; he looked, and the bush was blazing, yet it was not consumed. Then Moses said, "I must turn aside and look at this great sight, and see why the bush is not burned up." When the Lord saw that he had turned aside to see, God called to him out of the bush, "Moses, Moses!" And he said, "Here I am." Then he said, "Come no closer! Remove the sandals from your feet, for the place on which you are standing is holy ground."

The word of the Lord.

INTERCESSIONS

God of all life, your voice thunders in the wilderness and whispers in the flame that does not consume. We are called to bear witness to your word in our world. And so we pray: *Source of Life, may your life flow through us and bear fruit.*

- All the earth is holy ground. May we walk the earth in reverence. *We pray to the Lord.*

- Teach us to celebrate your majesty in the tiniest of creatures. *We pray to the Lord.*

- Empower us to share the burdens of the poor and the marginalized in solidarity and joy. *We pray to the Lord.*

THE LORD'S PRAYER
With these petitions in our hearts, we pray as our brother Jesus taught us: Our Father . . .

SIGN OF PEACE
As a sign of peace, Living God, we offer to you our upraised hands in joyous recognition that every moment you are creating life and revealing your love. May your peace rest on us.

CLOSING PRAYER
God of justice, at the burning bush you called Moses to lead Israel out of captivity into freedom. May we be agents of your liberation for our world and all who inhabit it. We ask this in Christ's name. AMEN

WEEK FOUR

MONDAY EVENING

✝

Giver of Life, animate our hearts;
inspire us to renew your creation.

PSALM 84:1-4
℟ May we dwell in the house of the Lord all our lives.

How lovely is your dwelling place,
    O Lord of hosts!
My soul longs, indeed it faints
    for the courts of the Lord;
my heart and my flesh sing for joy
    to the living God.

Even the sparrow finds a home,
    and the swallow a nest for herself,
    where she may lay her young,
at your altars, O Lord of hosts,
    my King and my God.
Happy are those who live in your house,
    ever singing your praise.

Glory . . .

Establishing the Renewed Creation   Monday Evening

SCRIPTURE   John 20:11-12a, 13-16, 18a

But Mary stood weeping outside the tomb. As she wept, she bent over to look into the tomb; and she saw two angels in white . . . They said to her, "Woman, why are you weeping?" She said to them, "They have taken away my Lord, and I do not know where they have laid him." When she had said this, she turned around and saw Jesus standing there, but she did not know that it was Jesus. Jesus said to her, "Woman, why are you weeping? Whom are you looking for?" Supposing him to be the gardener, she said to him, "Sir, if you have carried him away, tell me where you have laid him, and I will take him away." Jesus said to her, "Mary!" She turned and said to him in Hebrew, "Rabbouni!" (which means Teacher). . . . Mary Magdalene went and announced to the disciples, "I have seen the Lord"[.]

The Gospel of the Lord.

REFLECTION
In your life, what are some experiences, incidents, or insights that have led you to say, "I have seen the Lord"?

INTERCESSIONS
God of hope, the risen Jesus met Mary in her despair and called her by name. Like Mary, we may be uncertain when you call our names—and you call us nonetheless. And so

we pray: *Source of Life, may your life flow through us and bear fruit.*

- Awaken in us the courage we need to speak your presence to the world. *We pray to the Lord.*
- You were with Mary in her grief. May we be steady companions to all who suffer in our world. *We pray to the Lord.*
- Mary thought Jesus was a gardener. Strengthen all who labor in fields, farms, and gardens. *We pray to the Lord.*

THE LORD'S PRAYER
With these petitions in our hearts, we pray as our brother Jesus taught us: Our Father . . .

SIGN OF PEACE
As a sign of peace, Living God, we offer to you our upraised hands in joyous recognition that every moment you are creating life and revealing your love. May your peace rest on us.

CLOSING PRAYER
God of surprise and delight, we thank you for the ways you show yourself to us in all creation. May we rest well and awaken to your voice calling us by name. We ask this in Christ's name. AMEN

WEEK FOUR

TUESDAY MORNING

✟

Giver of Life, animate our hearts;
inspire us to renew your creation.

PSALM 27:1, 4-6, 8, 13-14
℟ May we dwell in the house of the Lord all our lives.

The Lord is my light and my salvation;
   whom shall I fear?
The Lord is the stronghold of my life;
   of whom shall I be afraid? . . .

One thing I asked of the Lord,
   that will I seek after:
to live in the house of the Lord
   all the days of my life,
to behold the beauty of the Lord,
   and to inquire in his temple.

For he will hide me in his shelter
   in the day of trouble;

he will conceal me under the cover of his tent;
> he will set me high on a rock.

Now my head is lifted up
> above my enemies all around me,
and I will offer in his tent
> sacrifices with shouts of joy;
I will sing and make melody to the Lord. . . .

"Come," my heart says, "seek his face!"
> Your face, Lord, do I seek. . . .

I believe that I shall see the goodness of the Lord
> in the land of the living.
Wait for the Lord;
> be strong, and let your heart take courage;
> wait for the Lord!

Glory . . .

SCRIPTURE   Isaiah 60:1-5a

Arise, shine; for your light has come,
> and the glory of the Lord has risen upon you.
For darkness shall cover the earth,
> and thick darkness the peoples;
but the Lord will arise upon you,
> and his glory will appear over you.
Nations shall come to your light,
> and kings to the brightness of your dawn.

Establishing the Renewed Creation   *Tuesday Morning*

Lift up your eyes and look around;
>they all gather together, they come to you;

your sons shall come from far away,
>and your daughters shall be carried on their nurses' arms.

Then you shall see and be radiant;
>your heart shall thrill and rejoice . . .

The word of the Lord.

INTERCESSIONS

God of glory, we long to live in the light of your presence, together with all your renewed creation. And so we pray: *Wellspring of Hope, bestow on us your living wisdom.*

- Grant us holy hospitality to welcome all who respond to your call. *We pray to the Lord.*
- Teach us to cherish the creatures that we may find unlovely, for all are the work of your hands. *We pray to the Lord.*
- May all the world see your goodness in the land of the living. *We pray to the Lord.*

THE LORD'S PRAYER

With these petitions in our hearts, we pray as our brother Jesus taught us: Our Father . . .

SIGN OF PEACE
As a sign of peace, Living God, we offer to you our upraised hands in joyous recognition that every moment you are creating life and revealing your love. May your peace rest on us.

CLOSING PRAYER
Gracious God, today may we seek your face in all that we do. May our work be a reflection of the kindness you have shown. We ask this in Christ's name. AMEN

WEEK FOUR

TUESDAY EVENING

✝

Giver of Life, animate our hearts;
inspire us to renew your creation.

PSALM 122:1-9
℟ May we dwell in the house of the Lord all our lives.

I was glad when they said to me,
  "Let us go to the house of the Lord!"
Our feet are standing
  within your gates, O Jerusalem.

Jerusalem—built as a city
  that is bound firmly together.
To it the tribes go up,
  the tribes of the Lord,
as was decreed for Israel,
  to give thanks to the name of the Lord.
For there the thrones for judgment were set up,
  the thrones of the house of David.

Pray for the peace of Jerusalem:
  "May they prosper who love you.
Peace be within your walls,
  and security within your towers."

For the sake of my relatives and friends
> I will say, "Peace be within you."
For the sake of the house of the Lord our God,
> I will seek your good.

Glory . . .

SCRIPTURE   Luke 24:13-16, 28-32

Now on that same day two of them were going to a village called Emmaus, about seven miles from Jerusalem, and talking with each other about all these things that had happened. While they were talking and discussing, Jesus himself came near and went with them, but their eyes were kept from recognizing him. . . .

As they came near the village to which they were going, he walked ahead as if he were going on. But they urged him strongly, saying, "Stay with us, because it is almost evening and the day is now nearly over." So he went in to stay with them. When he was at the table with them, he took bread, blessed and broke it, and gave it to them. Then their eyes were opened, and they recognized him; and he vanished from their sight. They said to each other, "Were not our hearts burning within us while he was talking to us on the road, while he was opening the scriptures to us?"

The Gospel of the Lord.

Establishing the Renewed Creation   *Tuesday Evening*

REFLECTION
What questions would you ask Jesus over dinner at the end of the day? Which of his teachings enflames your heart?

INTERCESSIONS
God of pilgrims, you send Jesus daily to walk with us along our way. Likewise, you call us to accompany those who need us in their journeys. And so we pray: *Wellspring of Hope, bestow on us your living wisdom.*

- Help us to see your abundance in our daily bread. *We pray to the Lord.*
- Make us fierce protectors of the gifts of the earth, the food and drink that sustain us all. *We pray to the Lord.*
- Strengthen us in justice, so that the day will soon come when all may be fed from the bounty of the earth. *We pray to the Lord.*

THE LORD'S PRAYER
With these petitions in our hearts, we pray as our brother Jesus taught us: Our Father . . .

SIGN OF PEACE
As a sign of peace, Living God, we offer to you our upraised hands in joyous recognition that every moment you are creating life and revealing your love. May your peace rest on us.

CLOSING PRAYER

Lord of the cosmos, may we rest this night in the palm of your hand. Bless all who work the land for the good of humankind and the animals with whom we share our lives. We ask this in Christ's name. AMEN

WEEK FOUR

WEDNESDAY MORNING

✝

Giver of Life, animate our hearts;
inspire us to renew your creation.

PSALM 89:1-2, 5-7, 11-12, 14-15, 52
℟ May we dwell in the house of the Lord all our lives.

I will sing of your steadfast love, O Lord, forever;
   with my mouth I will proclaim your faithfulness to
      all generations.
I declare that your steadfast love is established forever;
   your faithfulness is as firm as the heavens. . . .

Let the heavens praise your wonders, O Lord,
   your faithfulness in the assembly of the holy ones.
For who in the skies can be compared to the Lord?
   Who among the heavenly beings is like the Lord,
a God feared in the council of the holy ones,
   great and awesome above all that are around him? . . .
The heavens are yours, the earth also is yours;
   the world and all that is in it—you have founded them.

The north and the south—you created them;
    Tabor and Hermon joyously praise your name. . . .
Righteousness and justice are the foundation of your throne;
    steadfast love and faithfulness go before you.
Happy are the people who know the festal shout,
    who walk, O Lord, in the light of your countenance . . .

Blessed be the Lord forever.
Amen and Amen.

Glory . . .

SCRIPTURE   Ezekiel 34:25-31
I will make with them a covenant of peace and banish wild animals from the land, so that they may live in the wild and sleep in the woods securely. I will make them and the region around my hill a blessing; and I will send down the showers in their season; they shall be showers of blessing. The trees of the field shall yield their fruit, and the earth shall yield its increase. They shall be secure on their soil; and they shall know that I am the Lord, when I break the bars of their yoke, and save them from the hands of those who enslaved them. They shall no more be plunder for the nations, nor shall the animals of the land devour them; they shall live in safety, and no one shall make them afraid. I will provide for them a splendid vegetation so that they shall no more be consumed with hunger in the land, and no longer suffer the insults of the nations. They shall know that I, the Lord their God,

Establishing the Renewed Creation   *Wednesday Morning*

am with them, and that they, the house of Israel, are my people, says the Lord God. You are my sheep, the sheep of my pasture and I am your God, says the Lord God.

The word of the Lord.

INTERCESSIONS

God of peace, your promise of harmony and safety in the restored creation is beyond our imagining. Yet we know your promises are trustworthy. And so we pray: *Renewing Spirit, guide us into your new creation.*

- Awaken our souls to the promise of your ecology, O God. *We pray to the Lord.*
- May we be a safe haven for the people, animals, and all you have entrusted to us. *We pray to the Lord.*
- Give us holy anger to stand firm against those who oppress others and abuse the land. *We pray to the Lord.*

THE LORD'S PRAYER

With these petitions in our hearts, we pray as our brother Jesus taught us: Our Father . . .

SIGN OF PEACE

As a sign of peace, Living God, we offer to you our upraised hands in joyous recognition that every moment you are creating life and revealing your love. May your peace rest on us.

CLOSING PRAYER

May the God of the covenant of the new creation guide our work today. Bless us today with the hearts we need to feel the advent of your new creation. We ask this in Christ's name. AMEN

WEEK FOUR

WEDNESDAY EVENING

Giver of Life, animate our hearts;
inspire us to renew your creation.

PSALM 145:13b-20a
℟ May we dwell in the house of the Lord all our lives.

The Lord is faithful in all his words,
    and gracious in all his deeds.
The Lord upholds all who are falling,
    and raises up all who are bowed down.
The eyes of all look to you,
    and you give them their food in due season.
You open your hand,
    satisfying the desire of every living thing.
The Lord is just in all his ways,
    and kind in all his doings.
The Lord is near to all who call on him,
    to all who call on him in truth.
He fulfills the desire of all who fear him;
    he also hears their cry, and saves them.
The Lord watches over all who love him.

Glory . . .

SCRIPTURE   John 21:4-14

Just after daybreak, Jesus stood on the beach; but the disciples did not know that it was Jesus. Jesus said to them, "Children, you have no fish, have you?" They answered him, "No." He said to them, "Cast the net to the right side of the boat, and you will find some." So they cast it, and now they were not able to haul it in because there were so many fish. That disciple whom Jesus loved said to Peter, "It is the Lord!" When Simon Peter heard that it was the Lord, he put on some clothes, for he was naked, and jumped into the sea. But the other disciples came in the boat, dragging the net full of fish, for they were not far from the land, only about a hundred yards off.

When they had gone ashore, they saw a charcoal fire there, with fish on it, and bread. Jesus said to them, "Bring some of the fish that you have just caught." So Simon Peter went aboard and hauled the net ashore, full of large fish, a hundred fifty-three of them; and though there were so many, the net was not torn. Jesus said to them, "Come and have breakfast." Now none of the disciples dared to ask him, "Who are you?" because they knew it was the Lord. Jesus came and took the bread and gave it to them, and did the same with the fish. This was now the third time that Jesus appeared to the disciples after he was raised from the dead.

The Gospel of the Lord.

Establishing the Renewed Creation   Wednesday Evening

REFLECTION

The disciples recognized the risen Christ in the abundant catch of fish. What does God's promise of abundance mean for you?

INTERCESSIONS

God of lavishness and plenty, your risen Son was recognized in a spectacular catch of fish, an outpouring of wisdom to the disciples going to Emmaus, in his gently calling Mary by name. You open our eyes to you in your overflowing gifts. And so we pray: *Renewing Spirit, guide us into your new creation.*

- Protect those who work in dangerous occupations for the good of all. *We pray to the Lord.*
- Help us dare to trust your promise of abundance in the new creation. *We pray to the Lord.*
- Enable us to perceive you in the gardener, the traveler on the road, or the helpful fisherman. *We pray to the Lord.*

THE LORD'S PRAYER

With these petitions in our hearts, we pray as our brother Jesus taught us: Our Father . . .

SIGN OF PEACE
As a sign of peace, Living God, we offer to you our upraised hands in joyous recognition that every moment you are creating life and revealing your love. May your peace rest on us.

CLOSING PRAYER
Sustainer God, we rely on you in our work and in our rest. Watch over us this night, and awaken us to a hopeful and abundant new day. We ask this in Christ's name. AMEN

WEEK FOUR

THURSDAY MORNING

✝

Giver of Life, animate our hearts;
inspire us to renew your creation.

PSALM 95:1-7c
℟ May we dwell in the house of the Lord all our lives.

O come, let us sing to the Lord;
  let us make a joyful noise to the rock of our salvation!
Let us come into his presence with thanksgiving;
  let us make a joyful noise to him with songs of praise!
For the Lord is a great God,
  and a great King above all gods.
In his hand are the depths of the earth;
  the heights of the mountains are his also.
The sea is his, for he made it,
  and the dry land, which his hands have formed.

O come, let us worship and bow down,
  let us kneel before the Lord, our Maker!

For he is our God,
> and we are the people of his pasture,
> and the sheep of his hand.

Glory . . .

SCRIPTURE   Isaiah 61:10-11

I will greatly rejoice in the Lord,
> my whole being shall exult in my God;
for he has clothed me with the garments of salvation,
> he has covered me with the robe of righteousness,
as a bridegroom decks himself with a garland,
> and as a bride adorns herself with her jewels.
For as the earth brings forth its shoots,
> and as a garden causes what is sown in it to spring up,
so the Lord God will cause righteousness and praise
> to spring up before all the nations.

The word of the Lord.

INTERCESSIONS

Author of all righteousness, show us the way to justice and peace so that your will may be done according to your Word. And so we pray: *Holy Wisdom, grace us with abundant hope.*

- Help us to remember that caring for our neighbor requires caring for the environment. *We pray to the Lord.*

Establishing the Renewed Creation   *Thursday Morning*

- Enable us to perceive all the ways that we can live more harmoniously with the environment and all of creation. *We pray to the Lord.*
- Strengthen our resolve to live each day in cooperation with the Spirit so as to renew the face of the earth. *We pray to the Lord.*

THE LORD'S PRAYER
With these petitions in our hearts, we pray as our brother Jesus taught us: Our Father . . .

SIGN OF PEACE
As a sign of peace, Living God, we offer to you our upraised hands in joyous recognition that every moment you are creating life and revealing your love. May your peace rest on us.

CLOSING PRAYER
O Spirit who causes the earth to bloom and bear fruit, help us this day to cultivate your world for the common good. We ask this in Christ's name. AMEN

WEEK FOUR

THURSDAY EVENING

✝

Giver of Life, animate our hearts;
inspire us to renew your creation.

PSALM 80:7-11, 14
℟ May we dwell in the house of the Lord all our lives.

Restore us, O God of hosts;
   let your face shine, that we may be saved.

You brought a vine out of Egypt;
   you drove out the nations and planted it.
You cleared the ground for it;
   it took deep root and filled the land.
The mountains were covered with its shade,
   the mighty cedars with its branches;
it sent out its branches to the sea,
   and its shoots to the River. . . .

Turn again, O God of hosts;
   look down from heaven, and see;
have regard for this vine . . . .

Glory . . .

Establishing the Renewed Creation   *Thursday Evening*

SCRIPTURE   John 15:1-2, 4-5, 7-9

"I am the true vine, and my Father is the vinegrower. He removes every branch in me that bears no fruit. Every branch that bears fruit he prunes to make it bear more fruit. . . . Abide in me as I abide in you. Just as the branch cannot bear fruit by itself unless it abides in the vine, neither can you unless you abide in me. I am the vine, you are the branches. Those who abide in me and I in them bear much fruit, because apart from me you can do nothing. . . . If you abide in me, and my words abide in you, ask for whatever you wish, and it will be done for you. My Father is glorified by this, that you bear much fruit and become my disciples. As the Father has loved me, so I have loved you; abide in my love.

The Gospel of the Lord.

REFLECTION

Jesus called God the vinegrower, cultivating the vines so they may bear more fruit. In what ways have you cultivated generosity and care for creation in your life?

INTERCESSIONS

Source of all love, as Jesus abides in you, welcome us also to live in your care so that we may become witnesses of your loving presence within creation. And so we pray:
Holy Wisdom, grace us with abundant hope.

- Teach us to perceive your beauty even in the tiniest of creatures. *We pray to the Lord.*
- Give us the grace to know we are intimately connected to one another and to all living creatures. *We pray to the Lord.*
- Fill us with the awareness that all forms of life are deserving of protection and care. *We pray to the Lord.*

THE LORD'S PRAYER
With these petitions in our hearts, we pray as our brother Jesus taught us: Our Father . . .

SIGN OF PEACE
As a sign of peace, Living God, we offer to you our upraised hands in joyous recognition that every moment you are creating life and revealing your love. May your peace rest on us.

CLOSING PRAYER
"I am the vine, you are the branches," says the Lord. Help us extend his care and healing of others in our lives. We ask this in Christ's name. AMEN

WEEK FOUR

FRIDAY MORNING

✝

Giver of Life, animate our hearts;
inspire us to renew your creation.

PSALM 123:1-4
℟ May we dwell in the house of the Lord all our lives.

To you I lift up my eyes,
  O you who are enthroned in the heavens!
As the eyes of servants
  look to the hand of their master,
as the eyes of a maid
  to the hand of her mistress,
so our eyes look to the Lord our God,
  until he has mercy upon us.

Have mercy upon us, O Lord, have mercy upon us,
  for we have had more than enough of contempt.

Our soul has had more than its fill
  of the scorn of those who are at ease,
  of the contempt of the proud.

Glory . . .

SCRIPTURE Habakkuk 2:1-3

I will stand at my watchpost,
  and station myself on the rampart;
I will keep watch to see what he will say to me,
  and what he will answer concerning my complaint.
Then the Lord answered me and said:
Write the vision;
  make it plain on tablets,
  so that a runner may read it.
For there is still a vision for the appointed time;
  it speaks of the end, and does not lie.
If it seems to tarry, wait for it;
  it will surely come, it will not delay.

The word of the Lord.

INTERCESSIONS

Good and gentle Lord, give us the fortitude to wait patiently for the flourishing of the new heavens and new earth, while at the same time we participate in their development by living lovingly in your creation. And so we pray: *Merciful God, renew your life in us.*

- Breathe new life in us so as to live in hope and according to your vision. *We pray to the Lord.*

- Enlighten us to the ways that we can participate in bringing about both climate justice and global justice. *We pray to the Lord.*

Establishing the Renewed Creation Friday Morning

- Infuse our hearts with a sense of awe and gratitude as we cherish each day in your creation. *We pray to the Lord.*

THE LORD'S PRAYER
With these petitions in our hearts, we pray as our brother Jesus taught us: Our Father . . .

SIGN OF PEACE
As a sign of peace, Living God, we offer to you our upraised hands in joyous recognition that every moment you are creating life and revealing your love. May your peace rest on us.

CLOSING PRAYER
Keep us confident in your promise of a new heaven and a new earth. Fill our hearts with hope for that day, and do not tarry, O Lord. We ask this in Christ's name. AMEN

WEEK FOUR

FRIDAY EVENING

✝

Giver of Life, animate our hearts;
inspire us to renew your creation.

PSALM 24:1-6
℟ May we dwell in the house of the Lord all our lives.

The earth is the Lord's and all that is in it,
   the world, and those who live in it;
for he has founded it on the seas,
   and established it on the rivers.

Who shall ascend the hill of the Lord?
   And who shall stand in his holy place?
Those who have clean hands and pure hearts,
   who do not lift up their souls to what is false,
   and do not swear deceitfully.
They will receive blessing from the Lord,
   and vindication from the God of their salvation.
Such is the company of those who seek him,
   who seek the face of the God of Jacob.

Glory . . .

Establishing the Renewed Creation   *Friday Evening*

SCRIPTURE   Matthew 5:1-10

When Jesus saw the crowds, he went up the mountain; and after he sat down, his disciples came to him. Then he began to speak, and taught them, saying:

"Blessed are the poor in spirit, for theirs is the kingdom of heaven.

"Blessed are those who mourn, for they will be comforted.

"Blessed are the meek, for they will inherit the earth.

"Blessed are those who hunger and thirst for righteousness, for they will be filled.

"Blessed are the merciful, for they will receive mercy.

"Blessed are the pure in heart, for they will see God.

"Blessed are the peacemakers, for they will be called children of God.

"Blessed are those who are persecuted for righteousness' sake, for theirs is the kingdom of heaven."

The Gospel of the Lord.

REFLECTION

Do some Beatitudes resonate more deeply with your experience? Why?

INTERCESSIONS

O gracious God, our brother Jesus called us to be peacemakers. Help us to cultivate relationships of harmony and healing within our communities of faith. And so we pray: *Merciful God, renew your life in us.*

- Sensitize us to those invisible but most vulnerable persons in need of a community's embrace. *We pray to the Lord.*
- Empower us to be instruments of your peace and comfort to those most harmed by the climate crisis. *We pray to the Lord.*
- Summon our best efforts to be agents of your compassion, and care for those whose basic needs go unmet due to environmental injustice. *We pray to the Lord.*

THE LORD'S PRAYER
With these petitions in our hearts, we pray as our brother Jesus taught us: Our Father . . .

SIGN OF PEACE
As a sign of peace, Living God, we offer to you our upraised hands in joyous recognition that every moment you are creating life and revealing your love. May your peace rest on us.

CLOSING PRAYER
Living God, in the Beatitudes, Jesus teaches us the contours of your new heavens and new earth. Chasten our hearts to embody his words of blessing. We ask this in Christ's name. AMEN

WEEK FOUR

SATURDAY MORNING

†

Giver of Life, animate our hearts;
inspire us to renew your creation.

PSALM 96:1-13
℟. May we dwell in the house of the Lord all our lives.

O sing to the Lord a new song;
   sing to the Lord, all the earth.
Sing to the Lord, bless his name;
   tell of his salvation from day to day.
Declare his glory among the nations,
   his marvelous works among all the peoples.
For great is the Lord, and greatly to be praised;
   he is to be revered above all gods.
For all the gods of the peoples are idols,
   but the Lord made the heavens.
Honor and majesty are before him;
   strength and beauty are in his sanctuary.

Ascribe to the Lord, O families of the peoples,
   ascribe to the Lord glory and strength.

Ascribe to the Lord the glory due his name;
   bring an offering, and come into his courts.
Worship the Lord in holy splendor;
   tremble before him, all the earth.

Say among the nations, "The Lord is king!
   The world is firmly established; it shall never be moved.
   He will judge the peoples with equity."
Let the heavens be glad, and let the earth rejoice;
   let the sea roar, and all that fills it;
   let the field exult, and everything in it.
Then shall all the trees of the forest sing for joy
   before the Lord; for he is coming,
   for he is coming to judge the earth.
He will judge the world with righteousness,
   and the peoples with his truth.

Glory . . .

SCRIPTURE   Isaiah 65:17-19, 21, 24-25

For I am about to create new heavens
   and a new earth;
the former things shall not be remembered
   or come to mind.
But be glad and rejoice forever
   in what I am creating;
for I am about to create Jerusalem as a joy,
   and its people as a delight.

Establishing the Renewed Creation   *Saturday Morning*

I will rejoice in Jerusalem,
   and delight in my people;
no more shall the sound of weeping be heard in it,
   or the cry of distress. . . .
They shall build houses and inhabit them;
   they shall plant vineyards and eat their fruit.

Before they call I will answer,
   while they are yet speaking I will hear.
The wolf and the lamb shall feed together,
   the lion shall eat straw like the ox;
   but the serpent—its food shall be dust!
They shall not hurt or destroy
   on all my holy mountain,
   says the Lord.

The word of the Lord.

INTERCESSIONS

Divine Wisdom, open up our eyes to behold your abiding presence in all of creation so that we may stand in awe before this earthly sanctuary where you dwell. And so we pray: *God of Life, we long to dwell in your new creation.*

- Help us to recognize that we are profoundly connected to one another across this planet. *We pray to the Lord.*

- Seed within us a welcoming spirit so as to encourage the well-being of all who dwell in our common home. *We pray to the Lord.*

- Instill a determination in us to educate others in the care and love of our planet earth. *We pray to the Lord.*

THE LORD'S PRAYER
With these petitions in our hearts, we pray as our brother Jesus taught us: Our Father . . .

SIGN OF PEACE
As a sign of peace, Living God, we offer to you our upraised hands in joyous recognition that every moment you are creating life and revealing your love. May your peace rest on us.

CLOSING PRAYER
God of all living things, as we strive to participate in your building up of the new heavens and new earth, let our actions bear witness to your promise. We ask this in Christ's name. AMEN

Establishing the Renewed Creation   *Saturday Evening*

WEEK FOUR

SATURDAY EVENING

✝

Giver of Life, animate our hearts;
inspire us to renew your creation.

PSALM 150:1-6
℟ May we dwell in the house of the Lord all our lives.

Praise the Lord!
Praise God in his sanctuary;
 praise him in his mighty firmament!
Praise him for his mighty deeds;
 praise him according to his surpassing greatness!

Praise him with trumpet sound;
 praise him with lute and harp!
Praise him with tambourine and dance;
 praise him with strings and pipe!
Praise him with clanging cymbals;
 praise him with loud clashing cymbals!
Let everything that breathes praise the Lord!
Praise the Lord!

Glory . . .

SCRIPTURE   Matthew 13:31-33

[Jesus] put before them another parable: "The kingdom of heaven is like a mustard seed that someone took and sowed in his field; it is the smallest of all the seeds, but when it has grown it is the greatest of shrubs and becomes a tree, so that the birds of the air come and make nests in its branches."

He told them another parable: "The kingdom of heaven is like yeast that a woman took and mixed in with three measures of flour until all of it was leavened."

The Gospel of the Lord.

REFLECTION

When have you experienced or witnessed surprising growth? How did you cooperate with it, or resist it (and why)?

INTERCESSIONS

Divine Wisdom, open our eyes to recognize the new creation growing within our communities wherever harmony and joy bind people in seeking a shared future of hope. And so we pray: *God of Life, we long to dwell in your new creation.*

- Instill in us a desire to participate in the building up of new heavens and a new earth. *We pray to the Lord.*

Establishing the Renewed Creation   *Saturday Evening*

- Through our actions, may others perceive the newness of life that you seed in each season. *We pray to the Lord.*
- Make us your instruments of inclusion, welcoming all into full communion with you. *We pray to the Lord.*

THE LORD'S PRAYER
With these petitions in our hearts, we pray as our brother Jesus taught us: Our Father . . .

SIGN OF PEACE
As a sign of peace, Living God, we offer you our upraised hands in joyous recognition that every moment you are creating life and revealing your love. May your peace rest on us.

CLOSING PRAYER
God of all living things, we ask your blessings as we rest. Restore us tonight and renew us to cultivate your ecology of gift and generosity. We ask this in Christ's name.
AMEN

Final Thoughts on Renewing Creation

We end this week beholding the coming of a new cosmos through resurrected eyes. The morning scripture readings paint a breathtaking picture of a joy-filled new day, when every tear has been wiped away. We are like Mary of Magdala, the apostle to the apostles, when we grasp that life triumphs over death on Easter morning. All things are transformed by God's unending gift of life.

This is the new life that is forming. Only when all are welcomed will we forge true community. On that day we will live in full communion with God. The evening readings from the Gospels depict with more clarity what our lives will be in God's ecology. Jesus teaches us that our community of graced generosity, like a mustard seed, begins as a whisper of love implanted in our hearts. It then flourishes into a spreading habitat of grace that shelters and nurtures all forms of life. God's ecology thrives as an ecosystem of mercy, where the merciful will be blessed and the pure of heart will gaze upon God.

What will life in the ecology of God look like for us? How will we live into our resurrection, restored to our proper place as children of God in the family of all creation? We know that the coming of God's ecology is not a linear march. Instead, like all growth and development, the ecology of God grows in season and out, with new shoots on established branches to be pruned by the Divine Gardener. Our responsibility as co-creators remains now, as it has been since the dawn of creation, to nurture the

Establishing the Renewed Creation 209

lives of the people who journey with us, to care for our common home, and to cultivate life in the garden of God. The everlasting stirring of the Spirit will be the breath of life that carries us into the heart of the Trinity to our common home.

CONCLUSION

CULTIVATING LIFE FOR RENEWING CREATION

Life's bounty and goodness, from creation through its renewal, have been the themes of *Living Prayer*. We can retrace our journey and harvest in the graces that we have received.

In Week One, the many voices of scripture, from prophets to psalmists to evangelists, direct our gaze to the wonders of creation. We stand in awe and gratitude. Whether we have journeyed on this prayer-pilgrimage with others or individually in the deeply affirming presence of the Living God, we have learned to relish creation in which "we live and move and have our being." The natural world and our human communities, at their best, proclaim the Creator's glory. We absorb created beauty and bounty through our senses, in vibrant sounds and vivid colors, through fragrances that fill our lungs, tastes that tickle our tongues, and in embracing one another. We are shaped by the goodness of creation wherever, whenever, and however it touches us.

Week Two enables us to reflect on the implications of our ruptured relationships. The readings convict humanity for our most egregious exploitations, which have nearly exhausted the planet's resources. The earth has become parched to the point of combustion because we have chosen self over solidarity. An unprecedented number of species face extinction. Human lives are traded for luxurious goods while barriers protect some from the costs of their indulgences. In our misguided use of human freedom, we continue to sin against God's ecology. None of us escapes the unjust structures that place money above people, fear of scarcity over trust in abundance, and hoarding over giving. These are sins against the integral ecology—God's ecology—that *Laudato Si'* brings into the light. When we sin against creation and reject right relationships, our actions yield devastating consequences, which fall so heavily upon the poor and the most vulnerable.

Weeks Three and Four together teach us that cultivating life to nurture a renewed creation cannot be delayed until some uncertain future date. In the risen Christ, we can begin cultivating God's ecology *today*. In this time when we are redeemed but still awaiting the renewal of the cosmos, we usher in God's ecology by living according to the principles of generosity and gift. In these turbulent times of human and climate suffering, the Spirit beckons us to convert to a new way of living together. To effect enduring change within our own spheres of impact, our internal and external responses must reinforce one another. As servant-cultivators in the cosmic garden, we care for our common home, particularly by emulating Jesus' actions and teachings, which proclaim the reign of God. Praying through the four-week cycle from creation to renewed creation supports our internal conversion and deepens our awareness of God's ecology. Prayer supports conversion by reinforcing our desire to make amends and to reestablish an interdependent ecosystem where all life flourishes. By praying the morning and evening hours, we intentionally heighten our sensitivity to the suffering in the world, noticing how injustice permeates both abused nature and ruptured communities. We water the newly planted seeds of our commitment to life through prayer and practice as contemplatives in action. Divine grace, regular prayer, and green ritual practices can nurture new life in us when we prioritize care for our common home and establish the common good as nonnegotiable.

From the birth of the cosmos, portrayed as the first morning in Eden, as people of God, we have been formed to participate actively in God's ecology. The principle and foundation for the ecology of God are radical self-gift—giving of ourselves for the life of the world and trusting that our lives will be embraced into the heart of the Living God. Let us resolve to live the prayer of our hearts so that God's ecology flourishes and bears great fruit. Let us "beat our swords into plowshares" to renew creation.

May we breathe gratitude to the Incarnate One for healing our alienations and redeeming the world. We ask the Spirit to spur our hearts to labor fearlessly for

God's ecology. Remaining within the Trinity's embrace, we cultivate a renewed creation for our common home. May God's ecology be birthed through the prayers of our lives and our living prayer.

APPENDIX

GREEN RITUALS AND PRACTICES

We live our lives as incarnated spirits, embodied souls sprung from God's creation, and we are called into new life by the Spirit of God. *Living Prayer* emphasizes that we are siblings to all that God has created. Our prayer, then, should touch us in body and spirit. In baptism we are signed with water and oil. In Eucharist we taste and smell the bread and wine that are Jesus' sacred body and blood. We may genuflect, or kneel in prayer, or make the sign of the cross, gestures that bring our bodies to prayer.

Here are a few suggestions of practices to accompany the *Living Prayer* cycle. This is by no means a complete list: "green prayer" is limited only by the imagination of the one praying.

1. If you are praying the full month of *Living Prayer*, consider planting a seed at the beginning of Week One. As it germinates and grows, notice the tender shoot of new life reaching toward heaven. At the end of Week Four, transplant the seedling to

a larger pot, a garden, or a forest where it might continue to glorify God.

2. Find a stone, rough or smooth, small enough to fit in your hand. As you recite the day's office, hold the stone in your hand to saturate it with your prayer. Carry the stone with you through the day as a reminder of the new creation that the prophets proclaim.

3. Say a rosary for the healing of the world. On each bead, breathe in the troubles and distortions of the world and hold your breath to let the Spirit within you cleanse and heal the turmoil. Breathe out peace to the world. Ponder with each decade the mysteries of creation, the interdependence of life, and the healing and restoration of creation in Christ.

4. Create an altar in your prayer space with the four classical elements (earth, air, fire, water) to symbolize all of creation. You might represent air with a feather, fill dishes with earth and water, and light a candle.

5. As we might imagine ourselves to be with the communion of saints in prayer, compose a "litany of earth saints" inviting various trees, plants, and animals to come join in our prayer. You might also name saints like Thomas Berry, Francis of Assisi, or Hildegard of Bingen—whoever represents earth's care and healing for you.

6. As you begin prayer, stand and imagine your "roots" sinking deep into the earth below. Extend your arms upward and send your "branches" into the sky. Sway with the gentle breeze.

7. Sit with a bowl of various kinds of fruit. Feel each piece, its color, texture, and fragrance. Contemplate it as a gift of nature for our sustenance. Pray for the people who have been involved in bringing it to your table.

8. Learn birdsongs, so you recognize the voices of your singing neighbors. Pray for our winged siblings.

9. Walk and pray in your travels instead of driving. Feel your body relax and stretch with each step. Feel the ground under your feet, and notice the variety of plants and other creatures along your way.

10. Burn sage or incense to rebalance and focus the energy of your prayer space.

11. Run your hands through the sand on a beach or in a small container. Notice the temperature, the texture, and the movement of sand in your hands, and how each grain participates in the designs you sketch upon it.

12. Fast for a day in solidarity with those who have no access to safe, fresh foods. Donate what you save that day to a soup kitchen or a community garden.

13. Sit in a natural setting and take account of the different kinds of plants and their varieties of shapes, colors, and scents. Watch the people around you and how they interact with nature. Note also the sounds you hear: people talking, leaves in the wind, skittering of creatures in the underbrush, or birdsong floating on the wind. Reach out and touch the bark of a tree or smell the leaves of a plant.

14. For a week or more, mark sunrise and sunset with a pause, noting the angle of the sun and how shadows and light shift the mood at these liminal times. Listen carefully to the world coming to life or settling to rest (or the night creatures beginning to stir).

15. To situate yourself in God's cosmos, learn the names of the planets and stars in the sky above your home. To glorify God's cosmos, you might also look for some of the photos from the James Webb Space Telescope.